HOW TO PASS

STANDARD GRADE
ENGLISH

Jane Cooper

Hodder Gibson

A MEMBER OF THE HODDER HEADLINE GROUP

For Kenny

Acknowledgements

The Publishers would like to thank the following for permission to reproduce copyright material:

Photo credits

'Macbeth' image (p 19) reproduced by permission of the Ronald Grant Archive; 'Hue and Cry' image (p 23) reproduced courtesy of Lumiere Pictures; 'Shrek' image (p 38) reproduced courtesy of Dreamworks SKG; p 44 © Bennett Dean; Eye Ubiquitas/Corbis (UB008300); p 54 © Jeremy Horner/Corbis (HR007832); p 60 © Gunter Marx Photography/Corbis (MX006700); Photo of Ian Dowie (p 66) © John Morrison.

Acknowledgements

Every effort has been made to trace all copyright holders, but if any have been inadvertently overlooked the Publishers will be pleased to make the necessary arrangements at the first opportunity.

Extracts from Question Papers are reprinted by permission of the Scottish Qualifications Authority.

'Timothy Winters' from Selected Poems for Children © Charles Causley and extracts from Boy – Tales of Childhood © Roald Dahl are reproduced by permission of David Higham Associates; 'Something I'm Not' (Local Colour) © Liz Lochhead by permission of Birlinn Ltd; extracts from Shadow of the Beast © Maggie Pearson, Hodder Children's Books; extracts from My Parents Kept Me from Children Who Were Rough © 1986 Stephen Spender.

Artworks by Beehive Illustration.

Cartoons © Moira Munro 2005

Although every effort has been made to ensure that website addresses are correct at time of going to press, Hodder Gibson cannot be held responsible for the content of any website mentioned in this book. It is sometimes possible to find a relocated web page by typing in the address of the home page for a website in the URL window of your browser.

Papers used in this book are natural, renewable and recyclable products. They are made from wood grown in sustainable forests. The logging and manufacturing processes conform to the environmental regulations of the country of origin.

Orders: please contact Bookpoint Ltd, 130 Milton Park, Abingdon, Oxon OX14 4SB. Telephone: (44) 01235 827720. Fax: (44) 01235 400454. Lines are open from 9.00–6.00, Monday to Saturday, with a 24-hour message answering service. Visit our website at www.hoddereducation.co.uk. Hodder Gibson can be contacted direct on: Tel: 0141 848 1609; Fax: 0141 889 6315; email: hoddergibson@hodder.co.uk

© Jane Cooper 2005
First published in 2005 by
Hodder Gibson, a member of the Hodder Headline Group
2a Christie Street
Paisley PA1 1NB

Impression number   10 9 8 7 6 5 4 3 2

Year   2010 2009 2008 2007 2006 2005

Cover photo from Image Bank/Getty
Typeset in 10.5 on 14pt Frutiger Light by Phoenix Photosetting, Chatham, Kent
Printed and bound in Great Britain by Martins The Printers, Berwick-upon-Tweed

A catalogue record for this title is available from the British Library

ISBN-10: 0-340-88801-6
ISBN-13: 978-0340-88801-8

CONTENTS

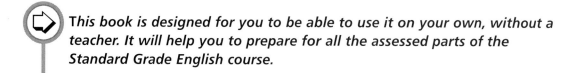

INTRODUCTION

This book is designed for you to be able to use it on your own, without a teacher. It will help you to prepare for all the assessed parts of the Standard Grade English course.

The book is particularly for you if you are aiming at Credit. You may be on the borderline between General and Credit and want to make the 'jump'. You may already be earning Credit grades some of the time but want to get them all the time. You may be getting 2s regularly but wish to aim for an overall 1.

This book will cover the three main assessed areas of Reading, Writing and Talk. You will find advice on how to tackle the Folio and your Talk Assessments, as well as the final Reading and Writing Exams.

There will be **exercises** throughout the book for you to try, and if you need **answers** for these you will find them at the back.

The Standard Grade English Course

What you will be assessed on

Let's start by looking at what is in Standard Grade English and what you will be assessed on. *Your overall mark is split up three ways* like this:

Just to complicate things, your mark can also be split up three ways like this:

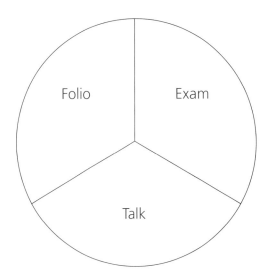

Just before the exam, think of this lower circle. By this time your teacher will have sent in your *Talk* grades, and your *Folio* will have been sent away and marked already. *When you go in to the Exam you already have two thirds of your marks in the bag.*

Your Exam itself tests *Reading* and *Writing*. *You'll find out in those chapters of the book what you actually have to do in the Exam.*

Key ideas

There are **two important ideas** you need to get your head round because they underpin the whole of this book.

The first is the idea of **distinction**. The marking scheme that teachers and markers use helps them to sort pupils into **Foundation**, **General** and **Credit**. It is actually not that hard to produce a decent General piece of work. There might be nothing badly wrong with the work and it might have few obvious mistakes. The marking scheme would say the work has 'overall adequacy', but it would not earn a Credit grade because there would be nothing there to make it **distinctive,** nothing that makes it **stand out in a good way**.

All through this book the advice you will find and the exercises you can try are designed to help you make your work distinctive. The poor, tired exam marker (whom you are about to meet) should find something in your work that makes her sit up and think, 'Hey that's different. That's fresh. I like it.'

The second key idea is about *skills*. Unlike some subjects such as History or the Sciences, *Standard Grade English is not full of facts to learn*. The exam, and the coursework, are not really intended to test your memory. *Instead you are being tested on your skills.* The best way to build these up is through practice. You will discover *in this book that there are lots of small techniques that you can use to increase your skills*.

Presenting your work

Before we go any further, it's time to meet an important person. In real life you'll never meet her, so here is a picture:

This is the marker. Be nice to her. She (and it is usually a she) is an English teacher who's either giving up her Easter holiday to mark your Folio, or else giving up her May evenings and weekends after being at school all day to mark your Exam. She has two weeks to mark either 170 Folios (that's 850 essays!) or about 600 Reading Exam papers, or about 400 Writing Exams. Look at her. She's exhausted. She's stuck at the kitchen table because it's the only one in her house big enough to spread out all the piles of work. She's eaten far too many biscuits and drunk too much coffee. It's midnight and she's still working. She does get paid, but not until July, and right now she's looking at your work.

The way you present your Folio can make her life much easier.

- ◆ Only write or type on one side of the paper.
- ◆ Write neatly when writing by hand and use a black or dark blue pen.
- ◆ If you can, type your pieces.
- ◆ When typing, never use a type size smaller that 12 point.
- ◆ Use a plain, clear font like Comic Sans, Helvetica, or Times.
- ◆ Set out your typing with double line spacing and use a double return to show that you are starting a new paragraph.

The marker is looking for the best in your work, but she is worn out. The easier it is for her to read your work, the easier it is for her to assess it thoroughly and carefully, and give you all the marks you deserve. Similarly, when you sit your Exams, keep your work neat and clear so she can see what you are trying to say.

What You Should Know

The GRC

To help her assess your folio, the marker uses something called the **GRC**. This stands for Grade Related Criteria. Basically, the marker has a list of details (the criteria) which describe what a pupil's work could be like. She relates these to your work, using them as a checklist and looking for the closest match. Once she finds this, she can give you a grade. Your class teacher also has a set of GRC he or she uses to grade your talks. Throughout the book phrases from the GRC will pop up to let you understand what you are aiming to do.

READING FOR THE FOLIO

When you write about a novel, story, poem, film or play, this is called **Reading**. I know that sounds odd. The full name for these essays in the Grade Related Criteria (GRC) is '**Extended Responses to Text**'. You will read and study the text, whatever it is, at school and then you will demonstrate your response to it by writing an essay to be sent off to the examiners.

The good news is that you do not have a literature exam. You only need to know and understand your text well enough to write about it in class.

Your teacher will mark your *first draft* and possibly discuss it with you before you *redraft* it. (By the way, one thing that makes Intermediate and Higher English so challenging after Standard Grade is that literature is part of the exam for these courses. You will need to learn all your notes and to be able to choose two suitable essay tasks by yourself to write in very little time in the exam.)

What goes in your Folio?

Key Points

Along with the W1 and W2 pieces discussed in the Writing chapter of this book, your Folio will contain three Reading essays. Over the two years of the Standard Grade course, you may write as many as nine or ten of these before finally choosing the best three to send away.

What You Should Know

The mixture of Reading essays sent away in your Folio has to follow certain rules:

◆ The *first* Reading essay in your Folio can be a Critical Evaluation of Poetry, Drama, or Prose. (Prose can be either a novel or a short story.)

◆ The *second* Reading essay in your Folio must be a Critical Evaluation of a text from a *different* one of the genres mentioned above.

◆ The *third* Reading essay in your Folio can be another Critical Evaluation of *any* of the three genres, **OR** a Critical Evaluation of Media, **OR** an Imaginative Response to Literature.

i **Most students end up submitting three Critical Evaluations and most of this chapter will be about how to write these.**

What You Should Know

Think of all the Reading Folio pieces you have worked on in school so far. Do you have enough pieces in the right balance of genres to be able to complete the reading part of the Folio yet?

It is very unlikely that you will get to choose which texts you study. Teachers do, however, try to pick texts that they are enthusiastic about and that they think their classes will enjoy.

You may get a choice of task when it comes to the time for writing your essay, though it is *more common for the whole class to tackle the same task*. Once all your essays are finished and your Folio is being put together (which will happen during about February or March of your fourth year) you will probably be given some choice of which essays you send away. *This choice should be discussed with your teacher and based on the grades he or she thinks the essays will earn*.

This may all sound as if you have little ability to influence the Reading part of your Folio. However what you can do is learn how to improve the quality of the essays you write. That is what we are going to look at now.

Critical Evaluations of Reading

Most or even all of your Reading essays will be **Critical Evaluations**. These are essays in which you show your understanding of, analyse and evaluate, a text that you have studied.

According to the Credit GRC, a Critical Evaluation should display *'a thorough familiarity with the text'* which is shown by *'analysis of its main ideas and purposes and through detailed reference to relevant areas of content.'*

Any book, or play, or poem really worth studying, anything your teacher picks to work on with your class, probably has several main ideas and themes running through it. The author may have had several purposes for writing it, several things he or she wanted to say.

Nobody expects you to analyse all of these in your essay. Although the GRC expect a Credit Reading piece to be 'substantial', that poor marker we met in the introduction does not really want to read essays that are thousands of words long because she has to mark over 500 of them!

Instead, you have to find one angle from which to study the text and, in your essay, only make detailed references to the areas of content which go with that line of study.

So, how do you know what to deal with in your 'detailed . . . substantial' essay? That is where the task comes in.

HOW TO PASS STANDARD GRADE ENGLISH

Now try this: Below you will see a number of tasks for Reading Folio pieces. Some of them are quite specific: they help the pupil to write about one aspect of the text they have read. Some of the tasks are very vague and woolly. Can you work out which tasks are specific and which are vague? The answers are at the back of the book.

◆ Having read Sillitoe's *Uncle Ernest*, discuss whether Ernest Brown is a dirty old man or a lonely innocent.

◆ Produce a critical evaluation of Wilfred Owen's *Dulce Et Decorum Est*.

◆ 'This dead butcher and his fiend-like queen.' Is this Malcolm's comment a fair way to describe *Macbeth* and his wife?

◆ Examine Golding's view of human nature as it is revealed in *Lord Of The Flies*.

◆ Analyse the riddles in Craig Raine's *A Martian Sends A Postcard Home*.

◆ Write a review of Steinbeck's *Of Mice And Men*.

◆ Show how, by the use of poetic technique, Browning lets us understand the mental state of the young man who describes himself as *Porphyria's Lover*.

◆ Review Harper Lee's *To Kill A Mockingbird*.

◆ In J. D. Salinger's *Catcher In The Rye*, how is Holden Caulfield's character revealed through his meetings with other people?

◆ *In Of Mice and Men*, how does Steinbeck show both the power and the weakness of dreams?

◆ In *A Time To Dance* by Bernard McLaverty, to what extent is Mrs Skelly a good mother?

◆ Review and evaluate *Stone Cold* by Robert Swindells.

Out of the twelve tasks, you should have found four vague and woolly ones. The first problem with these is that they don't give you any clear direction. You might just ramble on for several pages, doing nothing much more than retelling the plot. The second problem with vague tasks is that they don't tell that marker what you are supposed to be analysing, and she won't easily know what you are meant to be doing.

Now try this: Look back again at the tasks above. This time you can *ignore the four that you decided were too vague*. For each of the other eight, decide if the task is about **character**, *about* **theme**, or *about* **the writer's style**. Do any of the tasks ask you to deal with a mixture of these? The answers are at the back.

Hints and Tips

Before she starts teaching you any text, your teacher will probably decide what your final essay task will be. This means that the way you study the text will probably be tailored at least a little towards that final task.

Next time your English class starts a new text, ask your teacher what the essay task will be about at the end. Once you know, look out for extra details and ideas as you go through the work, so that when it's time to write the essay you have comments and observations of your own to add, as well as any your teacher might have led you to.

Structuring Your Essays

Because there are so many possible different reading tasks, there are many possible ways to organise your essays. You may find that your teacher gives you quite a detailed plan to follow. However, she may not. Or, you may be given plans for the first few essays you write and then be expected to plan the others on your own. Also, when you go on to Intermediate or Higher courses, you need to plan and write your own essays under pressure in the exam. It is important, therefore, that you learn to structure an essay for yourself.

HOW TO PASS STANDARD GRADE ENGLISH

Key Points

The basic structure for a Reading essay goes like this:

Paragraph 1   Introduction

Paragraph 2   Summary

Body of essay   Several paragraphs in which you deal with the given task

Final paragraph   Conclusion

Let's look at each of these steps in turn:

Paragraph 1: The introduction

Your introduction should do three things:

◆ Give the *title* of the text you have studied.

◆ Name the *author*.

◆ Make clear what your *task* is.

You can deal with the three elements of the introduction in any order and it is a good idea to *recycle quite a lot of the wording from your task descriptor* so that you head off in the right direction. There is no need, however, to do this in a boring way. Remember this is your first chance to grab the attention of that bored, exhausted, marker and to make a good impression on her from the outset.

Now try this: Look at the two introductions below. The two pupils are trying to start the essay about *Porphyria's Lover* from the list you have seen already.

Both introductions cover the three elements and both are clear. ***But why is the second one better?***

> My English class has just read a poem by Robert Browning called *Porphyria's Lover*. This essay will show how, by the use of poetic technique, Browning lets us understand the mental state of the young man who describes himself as Porphyria's Lover.

> As soon as I read *Porphyria's Lover*, I knew I was in the presence of a very disturbed narrator. Browning gradually reveals that young man's mental state by using various techniques throughout the poem. Exactly how the author does this will be the subject of my essay.

Have you decided yet what makes the second introduction better? Don't read on until you think you know.

The ***first introduction is very impersonal***. The writer talks about what her class has done, about what the essay will do, and about what Browning does. She does not say anything about what she thinks or what she will do. ***The second introduction is personal***. Right away, the student seems to be responding to what he has read. He says, 'I read,' and 'I knew.' Rather than making the essay sound as if it will do all the work, he again takes responsibility, calling it 'my essay.'

The first introduction is also weaker because it is ***dull***. It has a very predictable opening sentence. The second sentence takes the idea of recycling wording from the task instruction just a little too far, and just reproduces the whole thing. Just repeating all the same words in the same order makes the writer sound as if she cannot think for herself. This writer also repeats the name of the poem within a short paragraph.

For Practice

Look again at the eight interesting choices in the list of essay tasks above. I hope that at least one or two of them are based on texts that you have read. Try to write an introduction to fit one of these tasks.

Paragraph 2: The summary

A summary is a short way of telling a long story. This paragraph of your essay is there to give the marker a context. She may not have read the text you are writing about and she may not even know anything about it. A brief summary gives her a background for any references to the text you make later on in your essay.

The challenge is to **make your summary short**. It is too easy just to ramble. A summary should never be more than 100 words long. To prove that you can do this even with large and complicated texts, here is a 100 word summary of *Macbeth*:

> The play opens with Macbeth rewarded as a war hero. Three witches soon predict that he will go up in the world. These words start to come true but they also corrupt him and, under the influence of his ambitious wife, he kills King Duncan. Macbeth is an insecure king and protects his position by killing his best friend Banquo, many other supposed enemies and even innocent women and children. Further supernatural prophecies trick him into believing he cannot be killed but by the end of the play he and his wife are both dead.

This summary is just 95 words long, but all the main points of the play are there.

Making the summary fit the task

If you look back at the Macbeth task in the list above you will see that it uses the quotation, 'This dead butcher and his fiend-like queen.' The summary above would fit that essay well. The pupil has made quite clear that Macbeth kills people who do not deserve to die, which fits in with the idea of a 'butcher'. The reference to Lady Macbeth's ambition driving him to murder might count as an early example of her 'fiend-like' qualities.

For Practice

In 100 words or less, write a summary of a text that you know well. If you have studied any of the texts mentioned in the list of tasks earlier in this chapter you could write a summary of that text and try to 'spin' it slightly so that it fits the given task.

The main body of the essay

The Credit GRC say that throughout your Critical Evaluations you must demonstrate *'awareness of technique by analysis, using critical terminology where appropriate.'* Every paragraph in the main body of your essay has to demonstrate this awareness. I am going to teach you a technique that will allow you to analyse writers' techniques.

I call this 'going for a PEEE'. This does not mean that you'll be writing all your essays while locked in a toilet!

The letters *PEEE* stand for the three steps you should follow in every paragraph of the main body of your essay:

Step 1 Make a **P**oint which is relevant to your task.

Step 2 Back this point up with **E**vidence from the text.

Step 3 **E**xplain the **E**ffect of this on the reader.

To make sense of that, have a look at the following paragraph which has been written using the PEEE approach. The student is writing the *Porphyria's Lover* essay from the list you saw earlier and is dealing with the narrator's mental state.

One technique Browning uses to display the narrator's mental condition is contrast. After his description of the stormy weather which 'tore the elm tops down for spite' the narrator tells us that Porphyria 'glided' in and that 'She shut the cold out and the storm.' We see that although the speaker's mind is stormy, Porphyria, in contrast, is a calm and calming figure.

The first sentence makes a relevant point and introduces the technique of contrast. The second sentence actually uses not one but three short quotations to give evidence of the poet using this technique. The final sentence explains the effect of this technique on us, the readers of the poem.

For Practice

Below you will see another paragraph from the same essay. **Can you pick out the three steps? Highlight, label or underline them**. The answer is at the back of the book.

The writer also uses the weather in the poem to highlight the narrator's mood. In the opening lines of the poem the speaker describes the wind as 'sullen' and says that it 'tore the elm tops down for spite.' We realise of course that weather is not human and does not have moods. What we notice here is that the narrator is accidentally giving away his own moods. He is the one who is 'sullen' and will soon act out of murderous 'spite'.

If you are feeling really skilled and clever, you can construct your paragraphs so that all the three steps are covered, but in a different order. In a long essay, this ability to vary the pattern within your paragraphs shows real confidence and distinction.

For Practice

Read the following paragraph. This time the student is writing about William Golding's *Lord of the Flies*. Can you find the **P**oint, the **E**vidence, and the **E**xplanation of **E**ffect? The answer is at the back.

'Ralph wept for the end of innocence, the darkness of man's heart.'

Reading these words at the end of the novel, I realised that Ralph at least has learned something from the events on the island. His horrible experiences with the other boys, and his narrow escape from death at the hands of Jack's hunters, have enabled him to learn the lesson Golding explores in the whole book. Humanity here is shown as flawed, dark, and filled with the potential for evil.

Laying out quotations in essays

Look again at the paragraph above, from the *Lord Of The Flies* essay. You will see that the quotation at the start is set out slightly differently. It has been indented – moved in from the sides of the page. In the earlier paragraphs about *Porphyria's Lover* there was no need to do this, as the chosen quotations were very short, sometimes just a word at a time, and were woven into the pupil's sentences. However if you use a longer quotation, and certainly if you are using one or more whole sentences, you should place the quotation on a new line, and indent it.

After the quotation, if you are still carrying on the same paragraph you should go on to the next line, and start your writing at the beginning of the line. It would look something like this:

At the end of the battle, Macbeth pronounces his opinion on it:

'So foul and fair a day I have not seen.'

This is the first example in the play of dramatic irony. He does not realise what we know – that in his speech he is echoing words already used by the witches when they cast their spell.

Making sure you answer the question

In the main body of your essay, as well as following the PEEE format, every paragraph you write must be relevant to the task you are working on. Look back at the paragraphs from the *Porphyria's Lover* essay on page 14. Remember that the essay is about how the writer, Browning, puts across the mental state of the narrator. At the start of the first paragraph the pupil uses words that remind us of the task, referring to 'the narrator's mental condition.' Later in the paragraph the pupil again uses a phrase which firmly ties this paragraph to the task. She refers to, 'the speaker's mind'.

For Practice

Look at the second paragraph from the *Porphyria's Lover* essay. It is on page 14. Can you find the words which refer back to the task instruction? The answers are at the back of the book.

Writing in the present tense

It is an odd rule but, when you write about any text your have studied, you should use the present tense. The only time your essay should contain anything written in the past tense is when you are quoting directly from the text, since quotations of course must be exact.

For Practice

The writer of the following paragraph is trying the *Catcher In The Rye* essay from the list you saw earlier but her tenses are in a mess. Can you re-write it correctly? The answers are at the back of the book.

When Holden went to see his sister Phoebe he showed a different side of himself. Instead of being cynical he actually showed her how depressed he really was. It was obvious to me that Phoebe really loved him because she was so worried about him. When she asked Holden to make one thing he liked his only answer was that he liked Allie.

This answer helped me to understand not just that he was depressed, but perhaps also why: the only thing he liked was the brother who had been dead for years.

Your final paragraph – the conclusion

The Credit GRC say that you should give, **'a perceptive and developed account of what [you] have enjoyed in/gained from the text'** and that a Credit essay **'clearly conveys the sense of a genuine personal response.'**

As we have seen already in the well-written introduction to the *Porphyria's Lover* essay, it's possible to make your essay personal right from the beginning. Also, throughout the essay, whenever you explain the effect a technique has, you should make that part of the paragraph as personal as possible, showing what you have gained, or felt, or understood. When you get to your conclusion, however, you should make a special effort to give your personal response to the text.

For Practice

Look at the two concluding paragraphs below. Both pupils are trying to finish off that essay about *Macbeth*. Both include a personal response, but why is the second one better?

In this essay I have written about the play Macbeth by William Shakespeare. I thought this was a very good play. At first it was difficult for me to understand the language, but once I got into it I began to understand what the characters were saying. I liked the way the witches' predictions all came true, but never in the way that Macbeth expected them to. I did not like Lady Macbeth because she bullied her husband.

Having studied the play, and the Macbeths, in detail I feel that Malcolm's summary of them after their deaths is too basic. 'Butcher' might be a fair description of a man who has killed his king and ordered many other deaths, but there is more to Macbeth than that. His downfall is all the sadder if we remember the patriotic and loyal soldier he was at the start. I also feel that in believing the witches' prophecies and acting to carry them out he must have felt he was merely fulfilling his fate. Lady Macbeth too is more than a fiend. Yes, she may have said that she could dash out her own baby's brains if she had to. However when she actually becomes involved in a real murder this turns out not to be as easy for her as she might have thought. What she does haunts and destroys her. Although both perhaps deserve to die for what they have done, they do not deserve to be remembered the way Malcolm describes them.

Have you decided yet what makes the second conclusion better? Do not read on until you think you know.

The first writer again uses a very predictable opening sentence and tells the poor, bored, marker something that is obvious already. She also makes herself sound none too bright when she admits her difficulties with the language. The real problem, however, is with her personal response. All she does is tell us one simple thing that she liked about the play and one that she disliked.

Our second writer does much better because his conclusion is entirely made up of personal response. Most importantly, he fits his personal response to the subject of the essay. He uses the words 'butcher' and 'fiend-like' which were in the original task. Everything else he writes examines the two main characters and he gives his final conclusion on whether they deserve Malcolm's description, neatly tying everything in to the task once more.

For Practice

Go back to an essay you have written for your own Folio and read the conclusion. Now try to rewrite and improve it. Make sure that it is interesting, that it is all made up of personal response and that you fit that response to the task you were given.

Critical Terminology

*The Credit GRC say that you will use '**critical terminology where appropriate**' in your Reading essays and that you should be able to demonstrate an '**awareness of technique**.'*

Earlier in this chapter we looked at using the PEEE strategy to write the paragraphs that make up the main body of your essay. At the P stage when you make a point you are actually saying something about the writer's use of **technique**. Writers use many techniques, and not all of them have names. You can often just explain in your own words what the writer is doing such as: 'The writer uses a series of adjectives' or 'The writer uses weather to give us an insight into the young man's mental state.'

Many techniques, however, do have names and you will need to be able to use these confidently. These named techniques are most likely to be useful when you are writing about poetry. We are going to look at some of the most common techniques now.

First let's deal with some techniques of comparison and description.

Simile

A **simile** is a comparison using the word 'like' or the word 'as.' For example:

'Ears like bombs and teeth like splinters.'

Charles Causley

The two similes in this line help us to 'see' a boy with big round ears that look like the bombs in cartoons and broken, jagged teeth.

Here is another example:

'The law's as tricky as a ten foot snake.'

Charles Causley

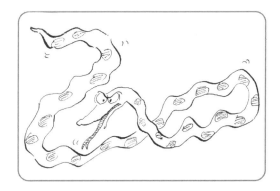

This simile shows us that the writer thinks the law is sneaky, hard to get to grips with, perhaps even dangerous.

Metaphor

In a **metaphor** the writer suggests that one thing is another.

This is not true, but it helps the author to make a strong comparison. For example:

'His hair is an exclamation mark.'

Charles Causley

We know the boy does not really have a punctuation mark on his head but when we read this line we understand that his hair must stand straight up on top of his head, just as an exclamation mark stands up on a line of writing.

'The golden hands with the almond nails.'

Liz Lochead

We know that the woman being described here does not have nuts where her fingernails should be. By calling her nails 'almond' the writer is telling us about the shape of the nails, a sort of pointed oval. This suggests to us that the woman probably takes care of her nails, not biting them or allowing them to get broken but filing and manicuring them into shape.

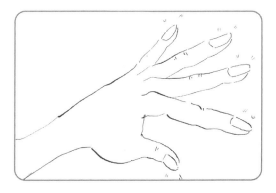

Key Points

Similes and **metaphors** can be used just to make descriptions more interesting. They can also be used to help us understand what some unusual object is like. They can help us see how a feeling affects the person feeling it, by making a comparison to something we can more easily understand.

For Practice

Read the poem by Stephen Spender. Can you find the following figures of speech? The answers are at the end of the book.

1 A *simile* that tells us the bullies were a noisy gang.

2 A *metaphor* that shows how much he was afraid of the boys.

3 A *simile* that shows how much the bullies' words hurt him.

4 A *metaphor* to explain how hurt he felt when they pointed at him.

5 A *simile* that tells us how strong they were.

MY PARENTS KEPT ME FROM CHILDREN WHO WERE ROUGH

My parents kept me from children who were rough
And who threw words like stones and who wore torn clothes.
Their thighs showed through rags. They ran in the street
And climbed cliffs and stripped by the country streams.   4

I feared more than tigers their muscles like iron
And their jerking hands and their knees tight on my arms.
I feared the salt coarse pointing of those boys
Who copied my lisp behind me on the road.   8

They were lithe, they sprang out behind hedges
Like dogs to bark at our world. They threw mud
And I looked the other way, pretending to smile.
I longed to forgive them, yet they never smiled.   12

Stephen Spender

Personification

In this figure of speech a **non-living, inanimate thing is compared to a living person or animal**. For example:

'That boat has killed three people'

George Mackay Brown

The writer makes the boat seem **alive**, **vicious**, perhaps even **evil**. He creates a much stronger effect than he would by just writing that three people have died because of the boat.

For Practice

Here is a short section from *Porphyria's Lover*. **What** is being personified? **How** is it being personified? The answers are at the back.

> *But passion sometimes would prevail,*
> *Nor could tonight's gay feast restrain*
> *A sudden thought for one so pale*
> *For love of her, and all in vain*

> Robert Browning

Now let's look at some sound effect techniques.

Alliteration

Alliteration is when a writer uses **two or more words close together that begin with the same sound**. For example:

> '*Something I'm not familiar with, the **t**une,*
> *of their **t**alking comes **t**umbling before them'*

> Liz Lochead

The writer is doing a very clever thing here. She is telling us that a sound has grabbed her attention. To do this she uses **alliteration**, a sound effect technique, to grab our attention and to make us notice what is happening in these two lines of the poem.

The main use of alliteration is often just that – to focus the reader's attention on a certain area of the text and perhaps to make us notice something else that is happening there, or to get us to concentrate on a point the writer is making.

Alliteration, however, can also affect the speed of a piece of writing. Alliteration made by repeating hard sounds such as b, k, t and so on can make the writing seem to speed up. For example:

> '*The runners **b**urst forward at the **b** of the **b**ang'*

Alliteration made by repeating soft sounds such as f, m or s can make the writing seem to slow down, and can produce a gentle feeling. For example:

> '*The **s**tream **s**lowly **s**lipped and **s**oftly **s**lithered between the trees.'*

Onomatopoeia

In this *figure of speech* the *sound* of the word helps us to understand its meaning. Most *onomatopoeic* words are connected to sound or movement. For example if you say the word '*splash*' out loud you can almost hear what a splash sounds like. The 'p' sound near

the beginning is the sound of the surface of the water being broken, the 'sh' at the end lets you hear the ripples moving out from the centre.

If you say the words '*thud*' and '*thump*' out loud to yourself they sound like exactly what those words mean, dull hitting sounds.

Assonance

You already know that when words end with the same sound this is called *rhyme*. You have just learned that when two or more words near each other start with the same sound this is called *alliteration*. *Assonance* is another technique based on *sounds within words*. In assonance, it is the *vowel sounds* in words that *sound the same*.

Example

The words '*cat*' and '*pan*' are an example of assonance because they both have the same 'a' sound in the middle. Assonance is about sounds and not spelling, therefore the words '*chute*' and '*boot*' also have assonance because they have the same sound in the middle, even though one word makes the sound with the letter 'u' and one uses 'oo'.

Like alliteration, assonance is often used to draw our attention to a certain part of the text because the author wants us to notice or think about something. Again, like alliteration, depending on which vowel sound is being repeated, assonance can make the text seem to speed up or slow down.

Example

For example:

*'The t**i**n h**i**t the r**i**m of the b**i**n and t**i**pped right **i**n.'*

The short 'i' sounds here make it sound as if the action happened quickly.

Now look at this example:

'He s**u**nk into his chair and sl**u**mped **u**nder the weight of the th**u**dding headache'

The repeated 'u' sounds here create a dull, slow, depressed mood.

Repetition

If a writer *uses a word more often than you would expect* to find that word being used normally in speech or writing, this is an example of *repetition*. For example:

'That moment she was mine, mine fair'

Robert Browning

By repeating the word 'mine' the speaker in this poem gives away the fact that he is possessive and obsessive.

The word might be repeated immediately, or there may be other words in between.

For example:

'No pain felt she:
I am quite sure she felt no pain'

Robert Browning

The speaker here has just committed murder. By repeating the words, 'no pain' he may be trying to convince us his crime was not so severe. He may even be trying to convince himself. Writers (or the narrators they create) repeat words to stress their importance and to create emphasis.

Read the poem by Liz Lochead.

LOCAL COLOUR

Something I'm not familiar with, the tune
of their talking, comes tumbling before them
down the stairs which (oh I forgot) it was my turn
to do again this week.
My neighbour and my neighbour's child. I nod, we're not on   5
speaking terms exactly.

I don't know much about her. Her dinners smell
different. Her husband's a busdriver,
so I believe.
She carries home her groceries in Grandfare bags.   10
though I've seen her once or twice around the corner
at Shastri's for spices and such.
(I always shop there – he's open till all hours
making good). How does she feel?
Her children grow up with foreign accents,   15
swearing in fluent Glaswegian. Her face
is sullen. Her coat is drab plaid, hides
but for a hint at the hem, her sari's
gold embroidered gorgeousness. She has
a jewel in her nostril.   20
The golden hands with the almond nails
that push the pram turn blue
In this city's cold climate.

Liz Lochead

For Practice

Can you find the following figures of speech? The answers are at the end of the book.

1 An example of *assonance* which emphasises how dull her clothes are. (Remember to look for sounds, not letters)

2 An *alliteration* to make us notice where the woman shops.

3 A *repetition* near the start to emphasise for us who the poem is about.

4 An *alliteration* to draw our attention to the neighbour's food.

5 An *onomatopoeic word* which means dull and actually sounds dull.

6 An *alliteration* which draws our attention to a very small detail of the woman's clothing.

7 A *near-repeat* of a *positive* word.

Word choice

Of course, every word a writer uses is chosen in some sense. Writers, however, make particular choices to use certain kinds of words that help them put across their message or tell their story.

One choice writers make is whether to use **formal or informal** language. Formal language is more suited to situations where the speaker or writer is trying to be polite, or is with someone who has authority over them. You would use formal language in a job interview, a letter of complaint, or if you were suddenly summoned to your Head Teacher's office. People often speak formally in awkward or difficult situations. Writing tends to be more formal than speech.

Informal language is more relaxed, slangier, and more chatty. You would use informal language when you are with your family or friends.

For Practice

Read the extract below. It is set in a funeral parlour where the dead bodies are referred to as 'Loved Ones'. A young woman who works there is speaking to Dennis, who has come to organise the funeral of a friend. Most of the time the woman speaks formally. *Can you find and underline the areas where she slips into informal speech?* The answers are at the end of the book.

'We had a Loved One last month who was found drowned. He had been in the ocean a month and they only identified him by his wrist-watch. They fixed that stiff,' said the hostess disconcertingly lapsing from the high diction she had hitherto employed, 'so he looked like it was his wedding day. The boys up there surely know their job. Why if he'd sat on an atom bomb they'd have made him presentable.'

'That's very comforting.'

'I'll say it is. How will the Loved One be attired? We have our own tailoring section.'

Evelyn Waugh

Writers can also choose whether to use **positive** or **negative language**. Look back again at the last few lines of the poem *Local Colour* that appeared earlier in this chapter. As the speaker begins to be more sympathetic towards and interested in her Asian neighbour she starts to use positive language. The words 'gold', 'golden', 'gorgeousness', and 'jewel' all have positive connotations.

For Practice

Read *Local Colour* again. Can you find examples of **negative** word choice in the poem? Answers are at the back.

Sometimes writers use **words connected to a certain subject**.

For Practice

You have already seen a few extracts from the poem *Timothy Winters*. The whole thing is on p. 30. *Can you find all the words connected to **war** or to **the army**?* The answers are at the back.

HOW TO PASS STANDARD GRADE ENGLISH

Timothy Winters

Timothy Winters comes to school
With eyes as wide as a football pool
Ears like bombs and teeth like splinters
A blitz of a boy is Timothy Winters   4

His belly is white, his neck is dark
His hair is an exclamation mark
His clothes are enough to scare a crow
And through his britches the blue winds blow   8

When teacher talks he won't hear a word
And he shoots down dead the arithmetic bird
He licks the pattern off the plate
And he's not even heard of the welfare state   12

Timothy Winters has bloody feet
And he lives in a house on Suez Street
He sleeps in a sack on the kitchen floor
And they say there aren't boys like him any more   16

Old Man Winters likes his beer
And his missus ran off with a bombardier
Grandma sits in the grate with a gin
And Timothy's dosed with an aspirin   20

The Welfare Worker lies awake
But the law's as tricky as a ten-foot snake
So Timothy Winters drinks his cup
And slowly goes on growing up   24

At Morning Prayers the Master helves
For children less fortunate than ourselves
And the loudest voice in the room is when
Timothy Winters roars, 'Amen!'   28

So come one angel, come on ten
Timothy Winters says, 'Amen
Amen, amen, amen, amen.'
Timothy Winters, Lord   32

Amen

Charles Causley

For Practice

Can you explain why Causley uses so many words about war and violence in this poem? What is he trying to tell us about Timothy's life? The answer is at the back.

Jargon is the specialised vocabulary that goes with a particular profession or a particular area of knowledge. Insiders very often use jargon to help them communicate quickly with each other but this can make non-specialists feel very left out or stupid. Technical and technological subjects seem to spawn a great deal of jargon.

For Practice

Read the following recipe. Can you spot the words which are *cookery jargon?* You'll find the answers at the back.

WHITE CHOCOLATE ICE CREAM

Take two 200 gramme bars of white chocolate. Cut off the last two rows of one bar and chop them into tiny pieces with a sharp knife to make 'chips'. Break up the rest of the chocolate.

Whip 15 fluid ounces double cream in a large bowl until it stands in stiff peaks, adding about one tablespoon of castor sugar towards the end of the whipping.

Separate four medium eggs. Whip up the yolks in a small bowl with a dessertspoon of warm water. In another large bowl whisk the whites until very stiff and peaked.

Melt the chocolate in a microwave, or on the stove in a bain Marie. Then take the chocolate off the heat and add the egg yolks and about two tablespoons of water. Beat well until you have a thick, glossy, yellow paste.

Pour this into the bowl of whipped cream. Spend a good long time folding this gently together until it's evenly blended. Tip the whole lot into your large bowl of egg whites. Gently fold together again until smooth.

Pour the whole lot into a freezable container. Sprinkle the 'chips' on top and freeze overnight.

HOW TO PASS STANDARD GRADE ENGLISH

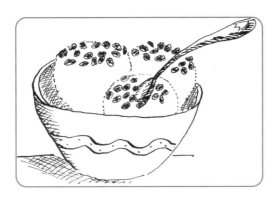

Because of the fresh cream this should be eaten within two or three days. It makes enough for about ten to twelve helpings. Just don't feed it to anyone who might be pregnant because of the uncooked egg in it.

By the way, if you feel like a break from study, the recipe really works and the ice cream is delicious.

Sometimes writers use words from a local **dialect** – the particular form of English spoken by people who live in or come from a certain place.

Read the following extract. The words come from an inscription on a rather tacky monument called 'The Lovers' Seat'. The seat is in Los Angeles, USA. Can you spot where the makers of The Lovers' Seat have tried to use Scots dialect? Answers at the back.

> This seat is made of authentic old Scotch stone from the highlands of Aberdeen. In it is incorporated the ancient symbol of the Heart of Bruce.
>
> According to the tradition of the glens, lovers who plight their troth on this seat and join their lips through the Heart of the Bruce shall have many a canty day with ane anither and maun totter down hand in hand like the immortal Anderson couple.

Evelyn Waugh

When a writer uses a number of words intended to arouse your emotions this is called **emotive language**. Words like 'terrifying', 'vicious' and 'evil' are much stronger and more emotive than words such as 'scary', 'aggressive' or 'bad'. Politicians, tabloid newspapers, and charities seeking your money are particularly fond of using emotive language.

For Practice

Read the following news article. *Pick out all the examples of **emotive** language. The answers are at the back.*

POLTERGEIST PETRIFIES STUNNED STUDENT

Shocking scenes occurred at a local castle yesterday when a schoolgirl working over her summer holidays was subjected to a terrifying ordeal.

Kate Carmichael (16) had been working at Castle Clegg for a mere three days when the horrifying events took place.

We understand that the castle's owners, Sir Gareth and Lady Alice Clegg had cruelly failed to warn Kate that the castle's dining room has long been the home of a vicious poltergeist known as 'Ranting Rachel.'

The appalling incident began when Kate was sent to the dining room to polish the contents of a canteen of silver cutlery. 'I had just finished the forks and started on the knives,' said the shocked girl to our

continued ➤

reporter. 'I left the room to get more polish and when I came back all the forks were lying in the fireplace. They were absolutely filthy again and covered in foul-smelling soot.'

Plucky Kate picked them up and was about to get to work on the forks again when she was startled by an evil cackling sound from the cupboard where the cutlery canteen was normally kept.

'I went over to have a look. I thought that perhaps it was the Cleggs' cat, Saint Olave. He's always getting trapped in places he's sneaked into.'

What happened next petrified the innocent teenager. As she touched the cupboard door she heard a mighty crashing sound behind her. Turning, she saw the disturbing sight of twenty place settings worth of knives, forks and spoons hurtling towards her at murderous speed. Callous screams now filled the air.

Kate's father Stuart told this paper later that he was 'totally and utterly sickened' by the attitude of the Cleggs when he came to the castle to collect his distraught and sobbing child. 'My girl was obviously suffering,' he said, 'and all they could do was worry about who was going to clean the silver in time for some fancy dinner they were having.'

Lord and Lady Clegg were unavailable for comment. However their estate manager, Alasdair Hicks, told us, 'This is just a ridiculous story put about by a hysterical young woman. Ranting Rachel is practically a member of the family. She might make a little noise now and again but she'd never do anything to hurt anyone. To suggest that she behaved in such a way is preposterous.'

Which *figure of speech* did the headline writer use? The answer is at the back.

For Practice

Several times in this chapter on reading for the Folio, I have mentioned or used examples from the poem *Porphyria's Lover* by Robert Browning. You are going to see the whole poem now. A young man narrates it in the first person. He kills the woman he loves in a rather inventive and horrible way. He does this because he is obsessed with her and because he does not think she loves him enough. In his madness he believes that killing her is the only way to free her from other distractions so that she can be his and concentrate on him.

Read through the poem. As you do so, **see if you can find examples of the figures of speech** we have looked at in this chapter. When you find one, **quote the example, saying which figure of speech is being used**. Try also to **explain** the **effect of each one**: what does it make you feel, notice or realise? What is Browning the writer trying to put across to us about the young man and his mental condition?

Madhouse Cell

PORPHYRIA'S LOVER

The rain set early in tonight,
The sullen wind was soon awake,
It tore the elm-tops down for spite,
And did its worst to vex the lake:
I listened with heart fit to break,   5
When glided in Porphyria; straight
She shut the cold out and the storm,
And kneeled and made the cheerless grate
Blaze up, and all the cottage warm;
Which done, she rose, and from her form   10
Withdrew the dripping cloak and shawl,
And laid her soiled gloves by, untied
Her hat and let her damp hair fall,
And, last, she sat down by my side
And called me. When no voice replied,   15
She put my arm around her waist,
And made her smooth white shoulder bare,
And all her yellow hair displaced,
And, stooping, made my cheek lie there,
And spread, o'er all, her yellow hair,   20
Murmuring how she loved me – she
Too weak for all her heart's endeavour,
To set its struggling passion free
From pride, and vainer ties dissever,
And give herself to me for ever.   25
But passion sometimes would prevail,
Nor could tonight's gay feast restrain
A sudden thought for one so pale
For love of her, and all in vain:
So, she was come through wind and rain   30

Be sure I looked up at her eyes
Happy and proud; at last I knew
Porphyria worshipped me; surprise
Made my heart swell, and still it grew
While I debated what to do.   35
That moment she was mine, mine, fair,
Perfectly pure and good: I found
A thing to do, and all her hair
In one long yellow string I wound
Three times her little throat around,   40
And strangled her. No pain felt she;
I am quite sure she felt no pain.
As a shut bud that holds a bee,
I warily oped her lids: again
Laughed the blue eyes without a stain.   45
And I untightened next the tress
About her neck; her cheek once more
Blushed bright beneath my burning kiss:
I propped her head up as before,
Only, this time my shoulder bore   50
Her head, which droops upon it still:
The smiling rosy little head,
So glad it has its utmost will,
That all it scorned at once is fled,
And I, its love, am gained instead!   55
Porphyria's love, she guessed not how
Her darling one wish would be heard.
And thus we sit together now,
And all night long we have not stirred,
And yet God has not said a word!   60

Robert Browning

Imaginative Responses to Reading

The third Reading essay in your Folio does not have to be a Critical Evaluation. You can instead put in an *Imaginative Response*. The text you are responding to must fit one of the three main genres of *poetry, drama or prose*.

You cannot submit an Imaginative Response to a media text.

Imaginative Responses very often take the form of either *letters* or *diaries*. *(For a closer look at the guidelines for these two types of writing, look in the Writing chapter of this book.)* Your teacher may ask you to imagine that you are a character in the text that you have studied and to write a letter or some diary entries from this character's point of view. The task might say something like:

◆ After reading *Of Mice and Men*, write George's diary entries from the day he and Lennie arrive at the farm until the day of Lennie's death.

Or:

◆ Imagine you are Sheila Birling from the play *An Inspector Calls*. Write to a friend, relating what happened the night that Goole unexpectedly arrived.

Key Points

To get a good Credit grade for an Imaginative Response, the marker has to see you doing two things. First, the GRC say you must display *'a thorough familiarity with the text'* by making *'detailed'* references to *'relevant areas of content'*, Second, the GRC say that you must also be *'confident and accomplished in the use of the chosen literary medium'*.

Detailed reference to relevant areas of content

This means that you must continually refer to details from the text. It is perfectly OK even to borrow words and phrases from the text, not putting them in inverted commas and showing them to be quotations, but instead weaving them into what you are writing as if they are the narrator's own words.

For Practice

Read the following extract from an Imaginative Response. The pupil had to imagine he was a doctor in the mental hospital where the narrator of the poem Porphyria's Lover has been locked up. Can you find the words and phrases the pupil lifted out of the poem to form part of the doctor's report? You'll find the answers at the end of the book.

Either this patient is a compulsive liar or else he is himself unaware of what the truth is. He is convinced that the victim was in love with him, but that she was too weak to set her struggling passions free and give herself to him forever. The patient insists that she had raced to his side that night after having a sudden thought of him so strong that it utterly distracted her from the gay feast she was attending. He feels she was compelled by love to come through wind and rain and visit him in his cottage. He believes that this proves Porphyria worshipped him.

For Practice

Look again at the whole text of *Porphyria's Lover* which was printed a few pages back. Carry on the doctor's report and describe the murder itself, lifting words and phrases from the poem to use as you go.

Confident and accomplished in the use of the literary medium

As well as proving that you are thoroughly familiar with the poem, play or item of prose that you have studied, the GRC say that you must also be **'confident and accomplished in the use of the chosen literary medium'**. In other words you have to actually be good at writing a diary, or a letter, or a short story itself, as well as being able to write one of these by basing it on a text you know. Imaginative Responses force you to use both your skills as a reader of literature, and your skills as a writer by showing that you are able to follow the conventions of a genre. You can find out about the conventions of and guidelines for different written genres in the Writing chapter of this book.

Critical Evaluations of Media

We have already seen that the third slot for a Reading Essay in your Folio can be taken by an Imaginative Response to Literature. You can also put in a Critical

Evaluation of Media. 'Media' here means a film or a TV programme: **you are not allowed to submit a Critical Evaluation of something from the printed media such as a news report or a magazine article**.

A Critical Evaluation of Media task might look like this:

◆ How does the animated film *Shrek* break the usual rules of fairy tales?

Or this:

◆ Show how the director of *The Sixth Sense* has filled the film with clues which might actually help viewers to guess the final twist.

What You Should Know

Critical Evaluations of Media are the rarest type of Folio piece. You may never get a chance to attempt one during your two years of Standard Grade English. Because you may never get the chance to try one, I am only going to say a little about these tasks here.

Critical Evaluations of Media are marked using exactly the same GRC as the ones used for assessing other types of Critical Evaluation. The marker expects you to use all your usual skills of understanding, analysis, and evaluation.

You should use the same essay structure that we examined earlier in this chapter, and should use the PEEE technique once again to build up most paragraphs in your essay. You also need to use the particular language and terminology of media in these essays. If you do not, you will lose marks.

For Practice

Out of interest, do you know what these media terms mean? Match the terms on the left to their correct meanings from the column on the right. The answers are at the back of the book.

1 scene	**A** all the elements which the viewer sees within a shot	
2 close up	**B** sudden change from one scene to another	
3 zoom	**C** clothing worn by the characters	
4 cut	**D** a shot focussing very tightly on an object or on the face of a character	
5 props	**E** a shot where all the action appears to be suddenly stopped	
6 mise en scene	**F** furniture and objects in a scene, especially objects handled by characters	
7 freeze frame	**G** sudden tightening of focus towards a close up	
8 soundtrack	**H** a short sequence of events happening in one place, or following one piece of action	
9 costume	**I** all the noises heard by the viewer, including dialogue, sound effects and music	
10 shot	**J** a sequence made without changing camera	

This is only a small selection of media techniques. Do not worry if you do not know them all. If your teacher does decide to get your class to try a Critical Evaluation of Media, he or she should teach you all the new terminology you need. *It is up to you to make sure that you use these terms, and that you do actually write about your text as a media item and not as if you had just read it the way you would a written document.*

THE READING EXAM

You will sit **two** Reading Exams. Every pupil in Scotland sits the General Exam. You will probably also sit the Credit Exam. The General is just there as a safety net in case you perform badly on the day. The examiner will mark your Credit paper first. If you pass that, she won't even need to read your General answers.

The Exam papers are made up of certain types of questions which come up year after year. In this part of the book you will learn about the most common or important question types, see some worked examples and have a chance to practise more on your own. All the examples are taken from real Standard Grade Exams, and when you are ready to check your work you will find the answers at the back of the book.

Before we go on to question types, let's take a look at some other important details in the exam paper.

The Layout of the Reading Exam Paper

Hints and Tips

Ask your teacher if you can borrow a Reading paper (both passage and questions) to look at or, if you have a book of past papers, get it out. As you read the next few pages of the book, keep the passage and questions from the Reading Exam paper open beside you so you can look at the details I am about to explain.

On the passage you will find the following helpful details:

◆ There is often a short line of introduction in *italics* telling you what the passage is about or where it comes from.

◆ If the passage originally came from a newspaper it will be laid out in newspaper style. (For a reminder of this, look at the section on Newspaper Reports in the Writing chapter of this book.)

◆ Each paragraph of the passage is individually numbered.

◆ The name of the author will appear. Do have a look at this so that you know whether to use 'he' or 'she' when you are answering questions about the writer and his or her techniques.

On the question paper you will find the following helpful details:

◆ You will see headings in **bold** telling you which part of the passage to look in for your answers. Until you see a new heading, all the questions you tackle will be from that same section or group of paragraphs.

◆ *Key or important words* in questions will also be picked out in **bold**.

◆ In the margin you will see how many marks are available for the question. If you see **2** and **0** separated by a little black square, then you have to get the whole answer totally right to get any points at all. When you see **2 1 0** then you may need to give two pieces of information. Or, if you are being asked to explain, you may get 1 mark for a partial explanation, but will need to explain more fully and in more detail to get both marks.

◆ The questions will take you through the passage in order, with the final questions asking you to think back over the passage as a whole.

◆ The amount of space your are given to write your answer in gives an indication of how much you need to write. If you run out of space (unless you have huge writing) you are probably waffling. If you leave a lot of the space empty and your writing is not microscopic then you may have missed something out or explained too briefly.

◆ If you are expected to give just one word or to pick from multiple choices, there will be a box to write in or tick.

The Language of the Reading Exam Paper

For Practice

Look at these words and phrases you might find in questions. Which expressions tell you that you ought to **quote** in your answer? Once you have worked this out, you can check at the back of the book to see if you were right.

Why do you think . . .?

Which word . . .?

Explain fully . . .

Find an expression . . .

How does the writer . . .?

Write down the word . . .

Which expression . . .?

By close reference to the text . . .

Unless you are sure you are being asked to quote, you should always answer *in your own words*. This is the only way to show that you really understand what the writer is saying.

For Practice

Below you will see a number of short extracts from recent Credit Reading papers. Can you rewrite each one, keeping the meaning but using your own words? For example: '**My mother drew in her breath**,' could become, '**My mum gasped**.' There will be some words you absolutely cannot change but you should change whatever you can without mangling the English language too badly.

- ◆ It was the 'n'-th year of preparations for a visit that always, in the end, failed to happen.
- ◆ Beneath her discreetly black coat my aunt had very long, slender, shapely legs.
- ◆ He was forever at a loss with guests.
- ◆ I examined my cousin surreptitiously.
- ◆ He ambled behind her to the escalator.
- ◆ He got the whole story of her financial hardship.
- ◆ The crew quickly came across a large bird, apparently flightless.
- ◆ Julian Hume believes the bird rooted at ground level, foraging fruits from palm trees and using its tough bill to break open and eat snail shells.
- ◆ Her perplexity was growing into an acute anxiety.
- ◆ In place of shoes his feet were bound with bandages.

You will often be asked to find an *expression*. This means either a single word, or else a *short* phrase, usually not more than about six words long. Be very careful with these. If the quotation you choose is too long and, even if it has the right expression somewhere in it, you may get no marks. This is because a long quotation, such as a whole sentence, will be made up of several different expressions and you will not have shown which of these is the one that fits the question.

When you are asked to make *close reference to the text* you may either use short quotations, or you may give examples from the text in your own words. You should make at least two references in your answer.

Question Types in the Reading Exam

In this section you will see an explanation, usually followed by some examples, and then some for you to try. The little bits of passage you need to look at are printed in a block on the left of the page, with the questions on the right. The answers are at the back of the book.

Questions asking you to obtain particular information from a text

These can be some of the most straightforward ones in the exam. Most exam papers also have a lot of marks available for this type of question. Look at the examples:

Behind them, all kinds of people are perched on the tailgates of a variety of vehicles. Is this some bizarre store for recycled rubbish? Well, in a way it is. In other words, you have found yourself in the middle of your first car boot sale.

Q 1 **Write down an expression which shows that the writer thinks this 'junk' makes a strange collection.**

A *bizarre store*

He waited at their corner, hands deep in pockets, his shoulder to the dirty, grey sandstone wall. The bell was ringing and he could hear the children streaming out into the playground. When she spotted him she broke into a trot and he retreated round the corner a little to swoop suddenly with a mock roar, bearing her laughing wildly up into his arms. As he set her down he asked quite formally what kind of morning she'd had. She began to speak, and her enthusiasm breathed upwards into his smiling face and beyond in the chill air.

Q 2 The man is shown to be thoughtful and caring towards his daughter. What evidence is there of this in the passage?

A *He makes her laugh, and he asks her about her morning at school.*

Now you try some examples:

The truth is that people will buy almost anything if the price is right. Old Playstation games, or genuine second-hand videos, will disappear as if by magic. Even more surprisingly, so will large, rickety (and empty) wooden boxes, elderly baseball caps that were given free with something ten years ago, shabby plastic dinosaurs that have been in many an imaginary battle and a pile of kitchen gadgets such as the tattie peeling machine that always took ages to wash afterwards, the expensive plastic containers with ill-fitting lids and the pancake mixer that liberally sprinkled you with batter every time you tried to use it.

Q 3 '. . . people will buy almost anything . . .' The writer gives several examples to prove this statement. Choose any **two** (APART FROM GAMES AND VIDEOS). In each case explain the writer thinks it is surprising that anyone should buy them.

We were in Dracula's castle sited on the remote Tihuta mountain pass where the Victorian Gothic novelist Bram Stoker based the home of his fictitious vampire – two days' carriage ride from Bistrita in northern Transylvania.

Q 4 Give two pieces of evidence which suggest that Bram Stoker wrote the novel *Dracula* more than one hundred years ago.

Downstairs was Count Dracula's coffin in a narrow vault, the walls painted with the dramatic scenes of human victims, wolves, skulls, skeletons and the black-cloaked monster himself, red blood dripping from his pointed fangs. Luckily we had decided to send their father down first as a guinea pig to test out how scary this experience was likely to he for our seven-, five- and two- year-olds.

After the screams from the crypt, Matthew decided he would opt for a tour with the light on and I agreed. Even so there was a certain nervousness as we went down the stairs. Suddenly Matthew let out a blood-curdling scream and jumped a foot in the air. 'I've just seen a horrible blue hand with long nails, round the side of that door,' he screeched.

One vampire hand was quite enough for a seven-year-old. Time for a drink and an ice cream. As we walked up to the main lobby there was 'Vampire' red wine for sale, glass vials of red liquid, wooden stakes and probably some garlic stashed under the counter.

Q 5 **In your own words** explain fully why their father was sent down first.

Q 6 **Write down an expression** which shows that Matthew did not complete the tour.

Their visit to us was bad timing. We were having a very cold snap, and in another week – when our guests would have gone – it would be November, then December after that, with Christmas fir trees for sale in the village shops. We were to be their last stop before they flew home. I suppose we were a family obligation. Or were we really something else, a different kind of invitation to their travellers' curiosity . . .?

He was watching a grey-haired lady dressed in a sagging blue raincoat, probably in her sixties. There was something in her movements that was very tense, yet she moved slowly, as if she had been stunned by some very bad news.

She put down the avocados – three of them, packaged in polythene – as if she'd just realised what they were and didn't need them. He followed her as she made her way to the express pay-point and took her place in the queue. He stacked his empty basket and waited on the other side of the cash-points, impersonating a bewildered husband waiting for the wife he'd lost sight of. He watched her counting her coins from a small black purse. The transaction seemed to fluster her.

And yet the dodo is more than a cheap laugh: the dodo is an icon. It's a creature of legend, a myth, like the Phoenix or the Griffin. But it's a myth that really existed. A living creature so bizarre it didn't need the human imagination to think it up – and an enigma from the first moment human beings laid eyes on it a little more than 500 years ago.

Q 7 **According to the narrator, what were the two possible reasons for the relatives' visit? Answer in your own words**

Q 8 Quote the expression which best suggests why he followed her to the pay-point.

Q 9 In your own words, describe what the detective did to avoid being noticed at the pay-point.

Q 10 Which **two** words does the writer use to emphasise the strangeness of the dodo?

In 1598, the crew of the Dutch East Indiaman, *The Amsterdam*, were navigating round the Cape of Good Hope when a storm blew up. After three weeks adrift, their battered vessel came within sight of a tropical island, which they named Mauritius. The island was a God-send. It meant they could rest and repair their boat, but most importantly it meant the half-starved crew could eat.

The fateful encounter now unfolded. The crew quickly came across a large bird, apparently flightless. Then, unable to evade its captors, it was quickly seized by the sailors.

Round in shape with a plume of tall feathers, the bird stood about three feet high, the size of an overstuffed turkey or swan. Its wings were small and useless, its head surrounded by a hood of fine feathers giving it the appearance of a monk's cowl. Yet most distinctive of all was its unfeasible looking bill. It was huge and bulbous, possessing a business like hook at the end.

Q 11 What does the writer's use of the expression 'fateful encounter' tell you about the meeting?

Q 12 In your own words, what does the writer's use of the expression 'unfeasible-looking' tell you about the dodo's bill?

Questions asking you to grasp ideas or feelings implied in a text

With this type of question you are going deeper into the text, not just looking at facts and information but going into **feelings**. These may be the feelings of the characters in the text, or those of the narrator, or those of the writer. Look at the worked examples.

At the last corner before the school's street they both halted in an accustomed way and he squatted down to give her a kiss. She didn't mind the ritual but not outside the gates: her pals might see and that would be too embarrassing.

Q 13 '. . . but not outside the gates . . .' Explain in your own words why the daughter made this condition.

A *If her friends saw her dad kissing her she would feel uncomfortable about it.*

A shadow moved behind her in the car. Behind them both the driver was lifting half a dozen assorted white suitcases out of the boot. My mother drew in her breath.

Q 14 'My mother drew in her breath.' What does this tell you about her feelings?

A *She is surprised.*

Now try these examples:

One advert was targeted in a ring of red felt-tip pen. The introduction was in big bold italics: '**This time last year I was made redundant. Now I own a £150,000 house, drive a BMW and holiday in Bali. If you . . .**' He opened out the paper and refolded it to the front page to check the headlines.

Q 15 Why do you think one advert in the newspaper was 'targeted in a ring of red felt-tip pen'?

He kept walking, on past the pillar-box at the corner of their street. That one was definitely unlucky: nothing he had ever posted there had brought good fortune. No, he would carry on to Victoria Road whose offices and air of industry made it feel a more hopeful point of departure.

Q 16 Explain why the man chose to post his letter in Victoria Road.

My three brave boys looked at each other and Douglas, the middle one, ran from the room. The eldest, Matthew, who had been taunting his younger brothers about being scared five minutes earlier, went a bit white and looked like he was going to change his mind about the visit.

I'd expected he would look stolid, and assertive, and the very picture of glowing health. Instead the eyes in his pale face flitted among us, like a prying spinster's, missing nothing.

'Oh, we've been everywhere! Everywhere!' my aunt explained, pausing at the hatstand to remove her wide-brimmed hat. 'Paris. Como. Rome.' She crossed them off on those creamed, manicured fingers with their scarlet nails. 'Where else, now? Antibes, of course. And we saw a little bit of Switzerland. That was cold!' She walked ahead of us into the sitting-room and made for the fireplace and the crackling log fire. 'Capri. That was just heaven. And Naples, of course.'

My mother watched her from the hall. 'Of course,' she repeated, just to herself, under her breath.

You had to blend in, pretend to be one of them, but you also had to observe them, you had to see the hand slipping the 'Game Boy' into the sleeve. Kids wore such loose clothes nowadays, baggy jeans and jogging tops two sizes too big for them. It was the fashion, but it meant they could hide their plunder easily. You had to watch the well-dressed gentlemen as well – the Crombie coat and the briefcase could conceal a fortune in luxury items.

Q 17 'My three brave boys' Explain fully why this expression might be considered to be surprising.

Q 18 What does the last sentence tell us about Walter's character?

Q 19 Look at the last sentence. What does this suggest the mother thought of the aunt's tales of travel?

Q 20 Explain what concerns the detective had about kids.

Q 21 Explain what concerns the detective had about well-dressed gentlemen.

He took her back inside and they made the long journey to the top of the store in silence. For the last leg of it he took her through Fabrics – wondering if they might be taken for a couple, a sad old couple shopping together in silence – and up the back staircase so that he wouldn't have to march her through Admin.

Q 22 In your own words give two pieces of evidence which suggest the detective felt some sympathy towards the woman.

Questions asking you to evaluate the writer's attitudes, assumptions and argument

This is quite an unusual question type. Notice that here we are looking at what **the writer** is thinking and saying. We are not in the mind of a character or of any narrator the writer has created. You are most likely to find questions like this if the passage is factual, especially if it is a piece of journalism. Look at the worked examples:

As we walked up to the main lobby there was 'Vampire' red wine for sale, glass vials of red liquid, wooden stakes and probably some garlic stashed under the counter. As these tacky, souvenirs revealed, it wasn't the real Dracula's castle but Hotel Castel Dracula, a three-star hotel built in the mountains to service some of the nearby, ski slopes.

Q 23 **In your own words**, what is the writer's attitude to the various goods for sale in the hotel lobby?

A *She thinks they are touristy rubbish.*

Now try these examples:

Surely this ridiculous bird, fat, flightless and vulnerable, had simply been caught and eaten to extinction? Too weak or stupid to defend itself, too trusting of humans, the dodo had met its inevitable end. According to ornithologist Julian Hume the fat, comical appearance of the bird is grossly exaggerated. Julian has travelled to Mauritius to investigate what the bird was really like and how it lived. It is here that the only two complete skeletons of the bird exist which have proved just how misrepresented the dodo has been.

Q 24 Which one word sums up the writer's sympathetic attitude to the dodo?

The architecture (1980s mock castle) reflected the Dracula movies but the setting amid the dramatic scenery of the Tihuta pass is stunning. The 'castle' is circled by bats every night and the surrounding forests have more wild bears and wolves than anywhere else in Europe.

Q 25 **In your own words,** what is the writer's opinion of the setting of the hotel?

Questions about sentence structure

Sentence structure just means the way that sentences are put together. English has certain rules about this. You may not be aware of the rules but you will probably notice if a sentence is constructed in an unusual way. Often a writer will construct an unusual or even 'wrong' sentence to grab you attention, or to gain some particular effect.

So, whenever you get a question about sentence structure, take a good look at the sentence you are being asked about and ask yourself a few questions:

1 Is the sentence noticeably long OR noticeably short?

2 Is it a proper sentence or is it somehow incomplete?

3 Is it: a. making a statement?

    b. asking a question?

    c. exclaiming in surprise or anger?

    d. giving an order?

4   Does it have any unusual or very noticeable punctuation?

What does this punctuation do?

5   Is the sentence in an odd order? Are any of the words in unusual places?

Once you have thought through these questions, you should know what it was the examiners found interesting about the structure of the sentence, and you ought to be able to tackle the question.

Look at these worked examples:

So if you fancy trying a boot sale, just for the fun of it, here are a few ground rules for participating in this most rewarding game.

Go as a buyer first, if you can. Go early, if you are selling. Many car boot sales that advertise an opening time of 10 am are being set up by seven or eight in the morning. Beware of the antique dealers. They will surround your table at this early hour like wild dogs around a carcase. Invest in a cheap wallpapering table. You can sell out of the boot of your car, but if you have as much junk to get rid of as most of us do, you will need more space than the average hatchback can supply. Take a secure container for your money – preferably a money belt so that you can keep your takings safely about your person. Don't leave handbags lying around; car boot sales are hunting grounds for purse snatchers. Don't sell old electrical goods: they can be dangerous, and you can be in trouble with the law for doing so. Take lots of food and drink with you: sandwiches, chocolate bars, flasks of tea and coffee, cans of soft drinks.

Q 26 The writer introduces the idea of giving practical advice. How does the sentence structure in the rest of this extract help to show this?

A   *Many of the sentences are commands. They are written so that they begin with a verb telling you what to do.*

Now try these examples:

Gingerly, he tried to reopen the envelope but it was stuck fast and the flap ripped jaggedly.

The transaction seemed to fluster her, as if she might not have enough money to pay for the few things she'd bought. A tin of lentil soup. An individual chicken pie. One solitary tomato. Maybe she did need the avocados – or something else.

Q 27 How does the structure of this sentence emphasise the man's care in opening the envelope?

Q 28 How does the writer emphasise that the woman had bought 'few things' through the use of sentence structure?

Questions about punctuation

There is rather an overlap here with questions about sentence structure since *punctuation is used to shape sentences and to organise the words within them*. However, you may also get more specific questions about the use of punctuation marks. First, have a look at the following notes about some of the marks you may be asked about:

. . . **ellipsis** dots used to tail off a sentence or to show gaps in speech or writing.

: **colon** often used to introduce a list, a quotation, an idea, information, an explanation or a statement.

– **dash** can be used in a pair like brackets to set aside information which is not vital, or may be used singly to introduce a piece of information.

' ' **inverted commas** go round the exact words said when someone speaks **OR** go round the words quoted when a quotation is used **OR** can imply that something is only 'so called' and not genuine.

( ) **brackets** used to separate off information which is interesting but not vital. The writing would still make sense if the bracketed part was missed out completely.

Now try these examples:

After all there's a little collection of pressed glass over there that is so irresistible, and the old hand-knitted Shetland shawl that nobody seems to have spotted, and isn't that a genuine stone hot-water bottle lurking among the rubbish . . .?

Q 29 Why does the writer use ellipsis at the end of the final sentence?

It was now well into the rush hour: traffic gushed by or fretted at red lights and urgent pedestrians commanded the pavements and crossings.

Q 30 Why does the writer use a colon? Is it to introduce a quotation, to elaborate on an idea, or to introduce an explanation?

At the last corner before the school's street they both halted in an accustomed way and he squatted down to give her a kiss. She didn't mind the ritual but not outside the gates: her pals might see and that would be too embarrassing.

Q 31 Why does the writer use a colon? Is it to introduce a quotation, to elaborate on an idea, or to introduce an explanation?

We were in Dracula's castle – sited on the remote Tihuta mountain pass where the Victorian Gothic novelist Bram Stoker based the home of his fictitious vampire – two days' carriage ride from Bistrita in northern Transylvania.

Q 32 Why does the writer use dashes in this paragraph?

It wasn't the real Dracula's castle but Hotel Castel Dracula, a three-star hotel built in the mountains to service some of the nearby, ski slopes. The architecture (1980s mock castle) reflected the Dracula movies but the setting amid the dramatic scenery of the Tihuta pass is stunning. The 'castle' is circled by bats every night and the surrounding forests have more wild bears and wolves than anywhere else in Europe.

Q 33 Why does the writer put the word 'castle' in inverted commas?

The driver opened the back door of the taxi and my 'aunt', as we referred to her – really my mother's aunt's daughter – divested herself of the travelling rugs.

Q 34 What is the function of the dashes?

Questions about word choice

Certain words belong to certain subject groups. (Think back to the many examples of language connected to war and violence we saw in the poem *Timothy Winters*.) Some words bring up certain ideas in the mind of the reader, or create certain sorts of atmosphere.

Now try these questions:

The transaction seemed to fluster her, as if she might not have enough money to pay for the few things she'd bought. A tin of lentil soup. An individual chicken pie. One solitary tomato. Maybe she did need the avocados – or something else.

Q 35 How does the writer emphasise that the woman had bought 'few things' through the use of word choice?

The driver opened the back door of the taxi and my 'aunt', as we referred to her – really my mother's aunt's daughter – divested herself of the travelling rugs. She hazarded a foot out on to the gravel – in a pointy crocodile shoe – as if she were testing the atmosphere. She emerged dressed in a waisted black cashmere overcoat with a fur collar and strange scalloped black kid-skin gloves like hawking gauntlets.

Q 36 What impression of the aunt do you get from the writer's choice of the words 'divested', 'hazarded', and 'emerged' to describe her movements?

Questions about effectiveness

You will sometimes find a question asking how **effective** you find an aspect of the writer's style. It's almost a trick question, as the examiners have pretty much decided already that the writing IS effective. What they really want you to do is to explain why. (If you are feeling very sure, and very skilled, you can argue that the extract is NOT effective but you'll have to use a lot of good evidence to explain why you think this.)

Now try these:

It was easy standing here to recall the bustle of business life. It came to him how much he wanted it, that activity. It was more than just something you did to make money: It was the only life he knew and he was missing out on it, standing on the sidelines like a face in the crowd at a football game.

Q 37 Explain how effective you find the simile in this extract.

He told her to take a seat while he called security, but when he turned from her she let out a thin wail that made him recoil from the phone. She had both her temples between her hands, as if afraid her head might explode. She let out another shrill wail. It ripped out of her like something wild kept prisoner for years. It seemed to make the room shrink around them.

Q 38 Quote a comparison from this section which shows how emotional or upset the woman was, and explain how effective you find it.

Questions about meanings in context

In these questions you are asked to use the **context to help you give the meaning of a word or phrase**. There is a set pattern for how to answer these. You will get **one mark** for **giving the meaning**, and the **second mark for showing how you were able to work out that meaning from the context**. For example:

It wasn't often you had this kind of intuition about somebody, but as soon as he saw her looking at the seeds, he was certain she was going to steal them. He moved closer to her, picked up a watering can and weighed it in his hand, as if this was somehow a way of testing it, then he saw her dropping packet after packet into the bag.

Q 39 'It wasn't often you had this kind of intuition . . .' How does the rest of the paragraph help to explain the meaning of 'intuition'?

A *Intuition means that you sense or guess something. He guesses that she will steal the seeds and then he watches her doing this.*

Now try this one:

When the London dodo died, the animal was stuffed and sold to the Ashmolean Museum in Oxford. Taxidermy not being what it is today, over the next few decades the dodo slowly rotted until it was thrown out in 1755. All, that is, except the moth-eaten head and one leg.

Q 40 Explain how the context helps you understand the meaning of the word 'taxidermy' here.

Questions about how ideas are carried on

The question will ask you **how the rest of the paragraph carries on an idea introduced in the first sentence**. These questions are easy to answer and a quick way of earning marks. All you have to do is to pick out details from later in the paragraph which go with the ideas introduced in that first sentence. Look at the worked example:

Downstairs was Count Dracula's coffin in a narrow vault, the walls painted with the dramatic scenes of human victims, wolves, skulls, skeletons and the black-cloaked monster himself, red blood dripping from his pointed fangs. So far on our Romanian holiday, the only blood-sucking had been from the mosquitoes in Bucharest. Luckily we had decided to send their father down first as a guinea pig to test out how scary this experience was likely to be for our seven-, five- and two-year-olds.

Q 41 'Downstairs was Count Dracula's coffin in a narrow vault, the walls painted with the dramatic scenes' In what ways does the writer convey the 'dramatic scenes in the vault?

A *The writer uses a list of horrific images such as blood, fangs, wolves, skulls and skeletons.*

Now try these:

All the junk in Scotland meets your befuddled gaze: thousands of unwanted gifts, the 'wee something' for Christmas and the 'I saw this and thought of you' for your birthday (how you wish they hadn't); then there are the holiday souvenirs. In short, all the stuff with which we tend to clutter our lives and our cupboards has somehow ended up in one place, awkwardly arranged on a vast number of folding tables. Behind them, all kinds of people are perched on the tailgates of a variety of vehicles. Is this some bizarre store for recycled rubbish? Well, in a way it is. In other words, you have found yourself in the middle of your first car boot sale.

It was depressing to unlock the door of his cubby-hole, switch the light on and see the table barely big enough to hold his kettle and his tea things, the one upright chair, the barred window looking out on a fire-escape and the wall-mounted telephone. He asked her to take the packets of seeds out of her bag and put them on the table. She did so, and the sight of the packets, with their gaudy coloured photographs of flowers, made her clench her hand into a fist.

Q 42 'All the junk in Scotland meets your befuddled gaze' How does the writer continue the idea of 'junk'?

Q 43 The detective found the sight of his cubby-hole 'depressing'. Explain how the writer continues this idea in the rest of the paragraph.

Questions about linking

These questions don't often come up in Standard Grade but you will almost certainly meet them in Higher. The question will ask you how a certain sentence, or paragraph, acts as a link at a particular point in the passage. There is a simple, four-step method to tackling these:

1 Quote briefly from the linking sentence or paragraph.

2 Show how that quotation makes a link back to earlier in the passage.

3 Quote briefly again from the linking sentence or paragraph.

4 Show how this second quotation makes a link forward to what is to come in the passage.

It is easier to understand this if we look at a worked example:

The three witches in Macbeth, prancing and cackling round their cauldron, provide the accepted clichés of witch behaviour and taste. Alas the Macbeth witches have merely served to reinforce prejudice, rather than cast illumination.

So does the witch deserve her poor image?

It is probable that the Wiccan creed goes back to the dawn of religious belief, when cave dwellers peered out and saw wonder in the rhythm of the changing seasons. Early witchcraft was probably no more than a primitive attempt to make sense of the unknown.

Q 44 In what way can the single sentence be regarded as a link of the ideas within the article?

A 'Her poor image' refers back to the prejudiced ideas about witches mentioned already, such as those found in Macbeth. The question, 'Does the witch deserve . . . ?' introduces the next part of the passage, which is going to present a truer history of witchcraft.

You should have been able to spot the pattern there of quote, link back, quote, link forward.

Now try this one:

His father looked at the sweating horse, and after a pause he said that he would be alright. Howard could see he knew the berries weren't ready yet, like the ones behind the steading that they always picked; and he understood that this was a lesson being set up for him when he came home without brambles: not to tell lies. And there'd be another lesson behind this one, the real lesson: that his father had been right about that sort of new-fangled nonsense coming to grief.

In spite of this, he forgot it all and slipped through the racecourse fence.

Q 45 Explain how the one-sentence paragraph is an effective link between the paragraphs before and after.

A crowd mobbed round the grandstand where they served drinks and sandwiches. Then, as nobody paid any attention to him, he wandered out among the planes. They were fragile and dazzling. The air was full of roaring, the strange exciting smell of gasoline, and drawling voices talking of their kites.

Final questions

Just above the last few questions on the Exam paper you will find an instruction in bold telling you to: '**Think about the passage as a whole**'. After the heading will be between one and three questions. As the heading suggests, these questions draw on your knowledge and understanding of the whole passage.

To be able to tackle one of these questions you need to know the whole passage well, and to have worked through it using the step by step questions. It is therefore, not possible to give you a chance to practise these here. Of course, whenever you do a past paper in class, you will be able to have a go at this question type.

These questions can cover many different topics. You may be asked to look at the writer's style throughout the passage. For example:

From the passage write down an example of the writer's use of humour. Explain why it is effective.

Or:

Why do you think the writer makes frequent use of brackets throughout the passage?

You may be asked about characters in the passage, whom you will now know well, or about their feelings and reactions. For example:

Overall how do you think the writer feels about his experience with the humming birds? Support your answer by referring to the passage.

Or:

For whom do you feel more sympathy – Pelagia or Mandras? Justify your answer by close reference to the passage.

You may be asked to show your understanding of the passage by making a prediction. For example:

Consider carefully all you have learned about the store detective and the woman. Supporting your answer by detailed reference to the text, explain whether you think the detective will have the woman charged, or let her go.

There are many other possible types of question you may be asked in this final section of the paper. You should have noticed from the examples given above that **one thing many of them have in common is an instruction to justify or support your answer by referring to the text**. By this stage in the Exam you should know the text intimately, and be quickly able to pick out short quotations or references to back up what you say in your answer.

You will still meet questions in Reading papers that do not fit the categories covered here. There are simply too many different ways a question can be phrased for us to cover them all. However, you should now have a clearer idea of what to expect.

No doubt you will do lots of Reading Exam practice at school. You can also buy books of past papers to try in your own time. These do not always come with the answers at the back, so you may have to be very charming to your English teacher if you want him or her to look at your work and tell you how you've done!

WRITING: WRITING FOR THE FOLIO

Two of your five Folio pieces will be pieces of Writing.

The first one – known as **W1** – should EITHER be a piece in which you write to give information OR one in which you handle ideas by arguing your own point of view or by discussing a controversial or complicated topic. This second sort of W1 piece is usually referred to as *Discursive Writing*.

Example

An example of a W1 informative task might be:

'Explain how to carry out some task you are familiar with, such as baking a cake, changing a wheel, or training a puppy.'

Or:

'Write a biography of a famous person whom you know about, giving details of his or her life and career.'

Example

An example of a W1 Discursive task might be:

'Write a magazine article for parents to read, in which you outline the five most important rules for happy family life. Show clearly why you believe each rule is important.'

Or:

'Fair trade is the best way to help the developing world. Discuss.'

The second piece of Writing in your Folio – known as **W2** – should be EITHER a piece of Personal Writing OR a piece of Imaginative Writing (usually a short story).

Example

An example of a W2 Personal piece might be:

'Write about a time when you faced one of your greatest fears.'

Or:

'Write about a person who has made a big impact on you and your life.'

An example of a W2 Imaginative piece might be:

'Write a short story with the title *Alone*'.

Or:

'Write a short story set in the heart of a busy and frightening city.'

Of the two options for W2, it is likely that your teacher will strongly encourage you to opt for Personal Writing. We will cover the reasons for this later.

WRITING IN THE EXAM

The Writing Exam is one hour fifteen minutes long. Every pupil sits the same Exam, and what you write can earn you a Foundation, General or Credit mark, depending on how well you write it.

You will be given a twelve-page booklet. It contains about 20 choices, from which you only have to pick one. Don't be like Craig. Craig was a pupil of mine, who often got in trouble. He came up to me after his Prelim and said proudly, 'Miss, you'll be really pleased wi' me. I worked really hard in that exam.'

I was all set to smile encouragingly when he went on,

'Miss, I done all twenty of them!'

Most of the booklet is set out with a large photograph filling the left-hand page, and a choice of tasks on the right. The photo is meant to inspire you, give you ideas, or get your thoughts flowing. The best way to explain this is to show you an example. Turn the page and take a look at it now.

FIRST **Look at the picture opposite**

It shows a father and his sons at a football match

NEXT Think about sport and about families.

WHAT YOU HAVE TO WRITE

---

1. 'Like father, like son'

Write a short story which fits this title.

OR

2. Write about a family member who has had a big influence on your life.

Remember to include **thoughts and feelings**

OR

3. 'Young people should play team sports'

'Sport is necessary for a healthy life'

'Taking part in sports gives teenagers discipline'

Discuss the importance and value of sport in young people's lives.

The back page of the exam booklet has no pictures. Instead the tasks there are usually based on quotations. There is often a task inviting you to write the description of a scene suggested to you by an extract from a poem. For example you might find a task like this:

17. Describe the scene suggested to you by **one** of the following:

'The rain set early in tonight
The sullen wind was soon awake
It tore the elm tops down for spite
And did its best to vex the lake.'

Robert Browning

OR

'Music and yellow steam, the fizz
Of spinning lights as roundabouts
Galloping nowhere whirl and whizz
Through fusillades of squeals and shouts.'

Vernon Scannell

Although the exam is designed for pupils of all abilities, the tasks on the back page can actually be harder to do well. Nobody will penalise you for not picking one of them. Unless something on the back page really inspires you, it is often safer to stick to a task from one of the picture pages.

Understanding the purpose

In the Writing GRC, one of the first things the marker is told to look for is how well you meet *'the purposes of the Writing task.'* Put simply, *this means that* **you must do what the task tells you to**.

If you write a story when the task was supposed to inspire personal writing, or if you write about a personal experience when the examiners wanted you to handle ideas and opinions in a piece of discursive writing, you have gone off task. You can find yourself dropping down to a lower grade, even if what you write is actually quite good. Make sure you understand what it is you are being asked to do.

Once you have chosen your task in the Exam, write the number on your answer paper so the marker knows which task and purpose you are tackling.

Choosing personal writing

As the mock Exam questions earlier in this chapter show, the twenty or so options will cover a wide variety of genres. As well as the ones you have seen already you might also encounter letters and news articles, or a task that invites you to write 'in any way you wish' which could lead to still further genres.

Common Mistakes

DON'T write a poem. Not only is it actually very hard to write a good poem, everyone's idea of what counts as a good poem is very subjective. One person's heartfelt and sensitive outpourings can be another person's self indulgent rambling.

Hints *and* Tips

Although there are lots of genres available to you and, even though the rest of this chapter will include advice for dealing with a number of these genres, **if at all possible you should choose a Personal Writing task**.

Why? Because the experience of English teachers and markers all over Scotland shows again and again that pupils just do much better on Personal Writing tasks. This is because you will be writing about something you have thought about or talked about a lot.

For Practice

Look back at the example questions earlier on page 67. Which one(s) would let you write personally? The answers are at the back of the book.

Later in this chapter we will look more closely at the skills needed for Personal Writing. For now, just remember to make a habit of looking for the Personal Writing tasks. Most years, the exam will have around five of these for you to pick from.

Using your time in the exam

The markers use exactly the same set of GRC to mark your Exam Writing as they do to mark your Folio Writing. If you think how long you have probably spent in class writing and redrafting your Folio pieces, you will realise that time in the exam is very tight. In addition to being able to write well, you need to be able to do so to order, and under pressure.

For Practice

Below you will see the time of the exam broken down into four chunks. What do you think you will be doing in each of these slots of time? When you have worked it out, you can check the answer at the back of the book

5 minutes _____

5 minutes _____

1 hour _____

5 minutes _____

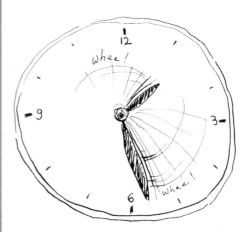

The only way to really get used to this is to practise against the clock. Your teacher will organise opportunities for you to do this in class.

GOOD WRITING TECHNIQUE

Paragraphing

Writing that is not correctly paragraphed becomes confusing, or even impossible to follow. Let's assume here that you do already know the rules for paragraphing. However, here is a brief reminder:

Remember the rule that if you are changing something in your writing you have to change to a new paragraph. This means that you need a new paragraph if you change:

- ◆ the place
- ◆ the time
- ◆ the speaker
- ◆ the character you are writing about
- ◆ what you are describing
- ◆ the idea that you are discussing
- ◆ the action that is happening

or if you make any other significant change. Any sentence starting with the word, 'Suddenly . . .' should also always be the beginning of a new paragraph.

Remember that you show a new paragraph in handwriting by taking a new line and moving your writing in a bit from the edge of the page. If you are typing, it's usual to use a double return to show a new paragraph.

For Practice

The following piece of writing is not in paragraphs. Write it out, correctly paragraphed. The solution is at the back of this book.

Monday was fine and sunny. There wasn't a cloud in the sky and I spent the whole day sunbathing. The next day was rainy and cold and I decided to go to the shops. At Intersport I chose a pair of trainers, a sweatshirt and some tracksuit trousers. When I went to pay the assistant said, 'That's two hundred pounds please.' 'How much?' I gasped. 'Two hundred pounds,' she repeated. 'Oh,' I gasped again. I dumped my shopping and ran off. On the bus home I felt really stupid. Why had I come without money? Suddenly, my fairy godmother appeared. 'I'll give you three wishes,' she said. 'Tracksuit trousers, trainers and sweatshirt please,' I replied.

Chapter 5

Speech marks

Once again, this is an area where you should already know the rules. As with paragraphing, poor use of speech marks makes writing hard to follow and really puts the reader off. There are three, basic, important rules to remember when you are using speech marks. Using these rules correctly will remove almost all the mistakes that hold back understanding.

The three basic rules are:

1 Put the speech marks round the actual words the person says:

'I need a doctor.'

2 Take a new paragraph when you are about to change who is speaking:

'I need a doctor'

'I'm a doctor'

3 The words that tell the reader who is speaking go in the same paragraph as the words that speaker says:

'I need a doctor,' said the woman as she came into Casualty.

Dr Brown rushed to her side, 'I'm a doctor.'

For Practice

Use the rules above to punctuate the following story. You can check the answers at the back of the book.

The two of them were on their way to the pictures when the argument broke out. Donna didn't want to see an action film. I hate them she moaned. Well I'm tired of always seeing romances answered Lesley. I don't care replied Donna. I want to see something that makes me feel happy inside. Suddenly Lesley said a very cruel thing. You only want to watch romantic films because there's no romance in your life. You haven't had a snog since we were in first year. That's not true! Yes it is! I had a snog with Graham after the Christmas party last year! No you didn't. You told everyone that you went off with him, but we all saw him at the bus stop on his own at the time when you said he was with you. This made Donna absolutely furious. At least I'm a bit choosy about who I snog. You've kissed so many guys your lips are fraying. Lesley couldn't think of anything to say in reply to this, and stormed off home in a huff.

HOW TO PASS STANDARD GRADE ENGLISH

There are, however, other, more complex rules, about the placing of commas and other punctuation marks inside the speech marks.

4   Any exclamation marks or question marks stay inside the speech marks.

'I need a doctor**!**' screamed the woman.

5   If the speaker's sentence should end with a full stop, but the sentence you are writing will carry on, finish the speech with a comma before the speech marks.

'I'm a doctor**,**' said Dr Brown.

6   If the sentence begins with words which introduce the speech, put a comma after these words and before the opening of the speech marks.

Dr Brown said**,** 'I'm a doctor.'

For Practice

Now use the more complicated rules (as well as those you have practised already) to punctuate this story. You will need to put in the questions and exclamation marks as well.

I need a doctor screamed the woman as she rushed into Casualty. I'm a doctor yelled Dr Brown, hurtling down the hospital corridor. What seems to be the problem. I've gone deaf said the woman. I woke up this morning and I wasn't able to hear anything out of my right ear. And she went on it tickles. Oh dear said Dr Brown. That does sound nasty. Let me take a look at it. He led her into a consulting room and shone a bright light in her ear. Hmm, yes he muttered. Do you have any children madam. I have a little boy, Liam. He's only four. But what has that got to do with my ears? Did you make him have peas for dinner last night. The woman nodded. I did, but I still don't see what this has got to do with me going deaf. And does he hate peas. Yes but I still don't understand the connection. Keep quite still said Dr Brown. You may feel an odd sensation but it shouldn't hurt. Ow yelled the woman, who certainly appeared to think that it had hurt. Aha! Exclaimed Dr Brown. He showed her the point of a pen lid, on which perched a slightly waxy-looking pea. I think your son got his revenge while you were asleep.

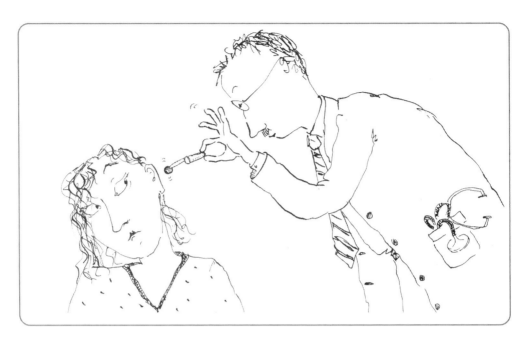

Using varied vocabulary

The Credit GRC expect you to use vocabulary which is **'accurate and varied'**. Any vocabulary which 'lacks variety' is liable to see you stuck with a General grade.

So how do you vary your vocabulary? Well, first of all, you need to have a wide vocabulary to draw on in the first place and there is no easy way to acquire this. It takes a long time, and you can only make your knowledge of words broader by reading and listening widely. Try listening to a speech-based radio station such as Radio Scotland or Radio 4 and reading quality newspapers like the *Scotsman*, *Herald*, *Guardian*, *Independent* or *Times*. Think about how the speakers and writers express themselves.

When you meet a word you don't know, look it up. If you don't understand the explanation, or you still don't feel that you could naturally use that word in any sentence that you would ever write or say, ask an adult.

You might even want to build a personal dictionary of new words. You can do this by getting a notebook or school jotter and writing each letter of the alphabet on the top right corner of a page. As you meet new words, write then down with their meanings. You might want to copy out the sentence where you found the word, or make up a sentence yourself using that word.

Even when you have a varied vocabulary, you still need to remember to use it. There are some words in English that just seem to creep out all the time. You may not even realise you are overusing them. Here are a few of the usual suspects:

big	nice	good	quite
said	get/getting/got		people

For Practice

Jot each of these down on a piece of paper. Beside the word, see how many others you can write down that mean the same thing and which you could use instead.

For Practice

Below you will see a story. The writer keeps repeating **thing** or **things**. Rewrite this to vary the vocabulary. You may need to change a few of the surrounding words as well as the one you want to vary.

As I looked across the landscape of the alien planet I saw the **things** beginning to slither towards me.

The **things** were horribly ugly. Each one was round and purple. They had two long **things** coming out of the top of their heads, which they used to sense their way across the ground.

Instead of arms or legs they had big rubbery **things** coming out of the centres of their bodies. Little **things** dangled off these and brushed through the pink grass.

Now that I noticed it, the grass was pretty horrible too. It was full of tiny **things** wriggling about. There were other **things** hovering and flying over the grass, and over the surface of a nearby pond which was covered in scummy-looking green **things**.

Things were looking pretty bad for me. The **thing** was, I was stuck here. My spaceship was malfunctioning and it was obviously going to take several days to fix the **thing**.

I decided that the best **thing to do** was to look in my ship for the right **thing** to use to begin the repairs. I got a big heavy **thing** and started to hit the **thing** on the underneath of my ship with it. It opened up and then I realised what the problem was. Lots of little **things** fell out on to the ground.

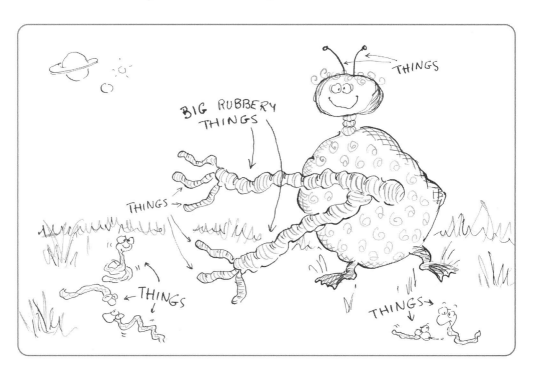

Just before we leave the topic of varying vocabulary, one final warning. In essays where you are following a strong structure, it can be easy to slip into beginning too many sentences or paragraphs the same way. If you are writing about the positive and negative sides of Macbeth's character for instance, try to avoid repeating 'Another good aspect of Macbeth is . . .' If you are writing a discursive or persuasive essay, watch out for too many phrases along the lines of 'Some people think . . .' or 'Another important point is . . .' Repeating phrases and patterns can be just as dull as repeating individual words.

EXPRESSING YOURSELF CLEARLY

The Credit GRC say that your sentence construction must be 'accurate'. To help you be aware of writing better sentences, we are going to focus on some short extracts of real writing by pupils aiming for Credit. All the extracts were produced under pressure during practice Writing exams.

For Practice

In these examples, some of the things pupils have punctuated as sentences are not really sentences. The underlined groups of words are not sentences because they do not contain a main verb and they do not make sense on their own. Try to rewrite each one so that it makes sense. You may wish to change some other parts of the sentences slightly, as well as changing the underlined sections.

If you want a little help, look at the back of the book where you'll see one possible answer to item A below.

A I focused my lens to get a better look. _As the mums pushed the children on the swings_. He was leaning over the fence grinning. _Watching every move he took_. I realised he was up to something.

B The doll, which I named Emily, reminds me of her in many ways. _The pale skin with rosy red cheeks, four freckles on the nose and green powerful eyes like the sea calm one minute and dangerous the next and greyish hair the same colour as rain clouds._

C When I was seven my grandfather died. It brought on a lot of emotions for me. _Some I had never experienced before._

For Practice

In the next few items, the students have written long rambling lumps of prose. These lumps need to be broken down into several shorter sentences. Once again if you want a little help to get you going you can look at he back of the book where you will find one possible suggestion for rewriting item A.

A As I walked down the corridor to my first class on my first day of my new school, nervous but still excited and wondered if anyone would like me, and what would they think of me would I fit in.

B We were all cringing and the waiter came over to move us to another table and everyone was looking at us but we could not stop laughing it was so funny.

C Last November I had a really bad cold and a chest infection and I was in bed bored and trying to sleep when suddenly all I heard was a bang which set off the dogs who then started barking and I wished it would all just stop.

D If I was to win a large sum of money I would probably blow half of it on clothes big designer labels.

For Practice

This student has written too many sentences which are really short and make the writing sound abrupt. Some of them are also not true sentences. Try to rewrite this to make it both more fluent and more accurate.

There was a lot to do there. Around the back was a trampoline that was extremely bouncy. I could use it for hours. And how I did. It was later moved next to the fitness area. Makes sense. There was a building there as well. In it there was a swimming pool, a gym, and a place to rent videos. One night we rented Braveheart. Good film. One time we went out and climbed the hill. Nothing but fields all around us.

Chapter 7

WRITING IN PARTICULAR GENRES

Now that we have examined the Writing requirements for the Folio and the Exam, and have looked at some general skills for Writing, it is time to look at the particular skills needed for individual genres. This advice applies whether you are writing in that genre to produce a piece for your Folio, or whether you are writing in the Exam. Let's begin with the genre most people approach best, and get the best marks for.

Personal Writing

The Credit GRC say that your Personal Writing should have *'insight and self-awareness'* and that you should be able to *'express personal feelings and reactions sensitively.'* Let's look at how you can do this.

If someone asked you what the rules for Personal Writing were, what would you say? You might come up with a list something like this:

◆ Include your thoughts.

◆ Include your feelings.

◆ Use lots of detail.

◆ Use lots of description.

◆ The writing should be true (though a little use of exaggeration can be used to liven it up).

◆ Use personal pronouns like I, me, my, mine, we, us, our, ours.

◆ Make clear how the events, experiences and people you describe have affected you.

We are going to look now at the first four of these guidelines, and then the last one.

Thoughts and feelings

Your Personal Writing will come uniquely to life when you include your thoughts and feelings. No one else has access to these. Only you can tell the reader what was happening in your mind and heart.

Interestingly, students often write extremely well about the hardest events in life. If we go through sad, difficult or tragic events we are acutely aware of how we feel at the time. Also, while a happy event in the end may just become a happy memory, sad events affect and shape us, and we have to keep working with and processing the memories, thoughts and feelings that go with these events.

When writing about thoughts and feelings, don't just state what these were, but explore them too. Don't just tell the reader you were angry, but say why, and how that anger felt. Don't just tell the reader you were afraid, but say why, and show how that fear affected you.

In the Writing Exam you will often see the instruction **Include your thoughts and feelings**. Even if that instruction is not there, your thoughts and feelings still must be.

Detail and description

Think of a strong memory. Now close your eyes for 30 seconds and think about it again.

Could you see it? Could you hear it? Was there a smell, a taste or a texture?

Read the following detail. The pupil is writing about a very normal trip she made to McDonald's, not knowing that when she got home she would hear that her father had suddenly died.

> I was standing in the queue to get a burger. I remember a woman with long black hair and a lazy eye came in to the restaurant. She kept staring at me. She walked in from the street and straight towards me. She smiled and rubbed my shoulder and then she walked out. I thought it was funny at the time, but now I think she somehow knew what I was about to go through.

The details of what the woman looked like, and what she did, are made absolutely clear to us. We are able to picture them because they are so clear in the mind of the writer, and they are clear in her mind because the odd event in McDonald's took on more significance and meaning later.

Now look at the following description. It comes from the autobiography of the writer Roald Dahl. He is describing a very vivid childhood memory.

> The doctor was bending over me. In his hand he held a long shiny steel instrument. He held it right in front of my face, and to this day I can still describe it perfectly. It was about the thickness and length of a pencil, and like most pencils it had lots of sides to it. Toward the end, the metal became much thinner, and at the very end of the thin bit of metal there was a tiny blade set at an angle. The blade wasn't more than a centimetre long, very small, very sharp and very shiny.
>
> 'Open your mouth,' the doctor said. Like an ass I opened my mouth. The tiny blade flashed in the bright light and disappeared into my mouth. It went high up into the roof of my mouth, and the hand that held the blade gave four or five very quick little twists and the next moment, out of my mouth into the basin came tumbling a whole mass of flesh and blood. I was horrified by the huge red lumps that had fallen out of my mouth into the white basin and my first thought was that the doctor had cut out the whole of the middle of my head.

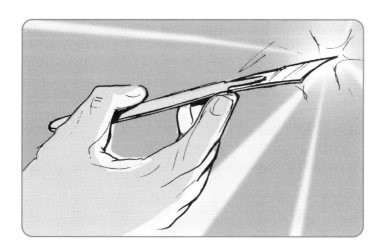

This happened when Dahl was eight years old. He did not write about it until he was in his sixties. After all these years, the surgical instrument, and the mass of flesh and blood tumbling from his mouth are still absolutely clear in his mind, and so he is able to write about them in detail.

Now take a look at the following two extracts. Both writers are describing the same event – a rock concert they went to together.

First they write about the band's entrance:

Writer number 1 When they finally emerged on to the stage, the crowd went insane. People were screaming and chanting, and there I was right in the middle of it all, speechless.

Writer number 2 All of a sudden a devilish red light lit up the whole stage. The fans went wild and the noise of heavy operating machinery just got louder to build the tension. Out of nowhere four light taps on the cymbal sounded, the curtain dropped and the band powered their way through their first song. Almost immediately the crowd surged forward and smashed me against the barrier. I gasped for air and couldn't get any as thousands of fans seemed to be ramming themselves forward.

Next they describe an incident during the concert:

Writer number 1 At the end of one of my favourite songs, the drummer stood up and launched his drumsticks into the crowd and my friend Johnny was lucky enough to catch one. As you'd expect everyone jumped up to grab them off him but one guy took it too far. The guy was huge and looked old enough to know better. He grabbed Johnny and stole the stick off him. In the midst of the mayhem there was nothing we could do to help.

Writer number 2 All of a sudden something came flying through the air and hit me right on top of my head. My reaction was to catch whatever it was. I looked down to see a drumstick right in the palm of my hand. Once again my luck was to run out. A fist collided with my cheek and I went over. A strong tugging was forcing the stick out of my hand. My eyes darted up to see a huge figure pull his fist back threateningly, forcing me to give up the drumstick, and leaving me with nothing but a bruised face.

You should be able to see that, though both writers are good, and while the atmosphere of the concert comes through in both pieces, writer number two makes better use of detail and description, especially when describing the band's first appearance on stage.

For Practice

Think of a time in your life when someone had to give you sad or bad news. Write one paragraph describing how that person looked and behaved as they broke the news to you.

Being reflective

One thing that will really raise you Personal Writing to Credit standard is the ability to be reflective. It is something that only mature and insightful writers are able to do. But what does it mean?

If you stand in front of a mirror you can examine yourself pretty thoroughly by looking at your reflection. Every spot and blemish will be visible, but you'll also be able to see all your good features and everything that you like about yourself.

That's the first meaning of being reflective in Writing – examining yourself. You may question and criticise yourself, or you may affirm yourself and realise that you handled the situation well. You may realise that certain experiences have shaped you and made you into the person you are.

For Practice

Now try this Here are a few reflective phrases to let you begin sentences or paragraphs in which you examine yourself. How many more can you add to the list?

'I realise . . .'

'I understand . . .'

'Because of this, I am . . .'

'Since this happened I . . .'

'I learned . . .'

Now think of the rear view mirror in a car. The driver can keep his or her eyes on the road ahead, but use the mirror to see what is happening behind.

That's the second meaning of being reflective in Writing – looking back. Often events in our lives make much more sense once they are over and we are older and wiser.

For Practice

Here are a few reflective phrases to let you begin sentences or paragraphs in which you look back. How many more can you add to the list?

'Looking back . . .'

'With hindsight . . .'

'I should have . . .'

'I could have . . .'

'I wish . . .'

Of course, as well as reflecting on yourself, you can reflect on others. You can question the way people behaved, or show that you understand now why they did the things they did. It may be that you disagreed with someone at the time but you now realise they did the right thing. On the other hand, when we are young we sometimes accept the things adults do without question, but as we grow up we are not so sure about their motives. You may also be aware of how events and experiences have affected other people as well as yourself.

A good General Grade 3 writer, or a writer who gets a Credit 2, might have a clear section of reflection at the end of their piece of writing. However if you are aiming for a Credit 1 and trying to show the *'insight and self awareness'* mentioned in the GRC, you should be reflecting throughout your essay.

Building up a repertoire of personal experiences

Remember the advice to choose Personal Writing in the Exam? It is actually possible to build up a stock of personal experiences to write about.

Similar topics come round again and again. If you can think of one amusing experience, one sad or moving one, and one which lets you show off your abilities and achievements, then you will usually find that you can use one of these in the Exam.

One of my pupils put it like this just before her Exam: 'I've got my Gran getting Alzheimer's and having to go into a home. That's the sad one. I've got growing up above the pub for a funny one. I've got conquering dyslexia. That's my personal achievement story.'

For Practice

Can you think of three or four experiences in life that you could develop and reuse?

_____   _____

_____   _____

For Practice

Here are some tasks from recent Writing Exams which involve producing a Personal piece. Pick one and try to write it. Remember to give yourself just an hour and a quarter in total, and to follow the time structure you saw at the end of chapter four. You will notice that some of them remind you to include your thoughts and feelings. Whether or not the reminder is there, your thoughts and feelings should of course be present in what you write.

◆ Write about a single occasion when you had to make a choice between your family and your friends. (2001)

◆ Write about a time in your life when you were involved in something which made you feel **both excited** and **frightened** at the same time. (2001)

◆ Write about a time when you were in conflict with someone over a particular issue. Be sure to include your thoughts and feelings. (2002)

◆ Write about a time when you lost something special, making clear how you felt and why. (2002)

◆ Write about a time when you achieved personal success and achievement, concentrating on your thoughts and feelings. (2002)

◆ Sometimes in darkest winter, all we want to do is huddle up in front of the fire and . . . Write about a special memory of such an occasion. You should include your **thoughts and feelings.** (2003)

◆ Write about an occasion in your life when you were caught doing something wrong. Remember to include your **thoughts and feelings**. (2003)

◆ A view I will always remember. Write about **a place** which had this effect on you. (2004)

◆ Write about an occasion in your life when teamwork was vital. Remember to include your **thoughts and feelings.** (2004)

Imaginative Writing

According to the Credit GRC, this type of Writing needs to show **'development that is sustained.'** You need to have **'some skill in using the conventions'** of the genre in which you are writing. Since any Imaginative Writing you do is liable to be some sort of story, what the GRC really mean is that you have to be a skilled story writer, and that you need to be able to produce a piece of some length. Even if you are good at this, it is probably better to use this genre only for your Folio, but to stick to Personal Writing in the Exam because of the short time you will have.

The accepted conventions of a short story

All stories, whether they are novels or short stories, consist of three major elements.

Short stories deal with these elements **simply** but **skilfully**:

◆ They cover a short period of time, or deal with a single event in their **plot**.

◆ There are only one or two main **characters**.

◆ The action takes place in one **setting** or very few settings.

Types of plot

The most common one, and the **classic short story plot**, goes like this:

◆ At the **beginning** a situation or context is established.

◆ In the **middle** the main character faces and tries to deal with one or two challenges, problems, dangers, or opportunities.

◆ By the **end** the character has either successfully overcome these problems or at least has learned some life lesson or some lesson about himself or herself while trying.

Another common type of short story is the one where the writer uses **a 'twist' at the end**. At the very end of the story a piece of information is revealed which surprises the reader and may also come as a surprise to one or more of the characters. The twist may be used to punish an unpleasant character, or to let the underdog character fight back in some way. One of the best writers of this type of story was Roald Dahl. If you can read his story *The Way Up to Heaven*, you will notice a final twist in which a most unexpected person turns out to be a calculating killer.

If you can successfully create a twist in your story you are certainly showing skill in using the short story conventions.

A third way of plotting a short story, and one which also shows a considerable level of skill, is to use **a flashback**. In this kind of story you can grab the reader's attention right at the beginning of the story by starting with your main character involved in some kind of action or drama, or in the middle of an argument or an important conversation. You could even begin your story by writing the ending. After this, you go back to the start of the events which led up to this point. You then tell the story in order.

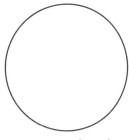

If you started your story at the end, and then flashed back to the beginning, then when you reach the place where you started, you can stop. In other words the plot of your story would go round in a circle like this:

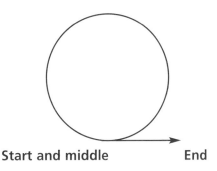

Start and end

If you started your story in the middle, then once you reach that point again you can go past it and on to the end of the story. Your plot would then look like this:

Start and middle   **End**

Choice of person and narrative style

Before you can start to write at all you need to decide how to narrate your story. The English language can be written or spoken in what are called three 'persons'

1   The **first person** is when the narrator is **speaking or writing about himself or herself**, or a group of people he or she belongs to.

2   The **second person** is for speaking or writing **to** somebody.

3   The **third person** is for speaking or writing **about** somebody else.

For Practice

To help you understand this, look at the words in the box below. Write a 1, 2 or 3 beside each word to show which person they belong to. You can check the answers at the end of the book.

I	your	us	he	you	his
me	her	she	them	they	our
we	mine	yours	theirs	hers	my

WRITING IN PARTICULAR GENRES

For Practice

Now look at this extract from *Shadow of the Beast*. It has been written in the third person. Rewrite it into the first person.

Troy got to his feet and, brushing the worst of the damp sand from his jeans as he went, set off after the men. He took long strides on the downward slope in his haste not to lose them, digging in his heels to keep himself from falling headlong, ignoring the cold sand spilling into his shoes. Instead of following the track down to the road, the men had chosen a footpath that snaked among clumps of bushes. One moment they were there walking in single file, then gone, to reappear much further on than he expected, and off to the right, where the path was barely visible. He thought he'd lost them altogether, then there they were, tramping across the first of the fields, bunched up again in twos and threes, the helmsman at their head.

Good beginnings

In a short story, your opening needs to grab the reader's attention straight away. You have to intrigue the reader, and make him or her want to read on.

For Practice

Read the two different beginnings for the same story, then answer the questions below. The answers are at the back.

Opening number 1 Michael got up and looked in the wardrobe. He always put the same jeans and sweatshirt on anyway. He put them on and went downstairs. He started to eat his breakfast. He had a piece of toast and jam and a cup of tea. He didn't even like tea. He looked for his jacket. He couldn't find his gloves or his homework for that nippy Miss Brumby. He suddenly didn't feel like going to school. He decided to skive. He would regret it later.

Opening number 2 Pretty soon after he got up Michael knew it was going to be another dull and disastrous day at school. He hardly realised that his skive would be nowhere near dull, but decidedly disastrous.

- What are the **weaknesses** of Opening number 1?
- What are the **strengths** of Opening number 2?
- Does Opening number 2 have any **weaknesses**?
- Does Opening number 1 have any **strengths**?

Realistic dialogue

It is really important to be sure that the dialogue you write sounds like real people talking. Always ask yourself if you can imagine anyone you know saying the words you write.

Of course some characters will speak more formally than others. Children and teenagers tend to use more slang than adult authority figures. People speak more or less formally depending on the situation. Believable dialogue matches both the characters you have created, and the situation you have put them in.

Mistakes to avoid

There are a few common mistakes that many pupils make. Beware of all of these:

- Rehashing the plot of a film you have seen.
- 'Padding' your story with unnecessary details: we do not need to know when your main character got up and what they had for breakfast, we just need to know the information relevant to the story.
- Writing without dialogue: a story must have characters speaking to each other or it will just never come to life. Make sure you know the rules for punctuating speech which you will find elsewhere in this chapter.

Bad endings

There are four forbidden endings:

- Any ending where it all turns out to be have been a dream or a hallucination.
- Any ending where the characters' problems are solved by an unexpected Lottery win or a sudden inheritance from a dead relative.
- Any ending which suddenly summarises all the events over a long period of time such as the whole of the next year, or the rest of the characters' lives.
- Any use of the words 'happily ever after'.

(!) Can you work out WHY each of these endings is forbidden? Why does each one lower the quality of your writing? The answers are at the back.

For Practice

Here are some tasks from recent Writing Exams which involve producing Imaginative Writing. Pick one and try to write it. Remember to give yourself just an hour and a quarter in total, and to follow the time structure you saw at the end of chapter four.

- ◆ *Write a short story* using the title: Older and Wiser (2001)
- ◆ *Write a short story* using the title: Life is Full of Ups and Downs. (2001)
- ◆ Write a tale of mystery and imagination. (2002)

Choose one of the following and continue the story:

> The map and instructions had been quite clear and he had faithfully followed them. Yet, here he sat not knowing what road to take and what the next step of the journey would hold.

OR

> She had waited and then waited again so many times but her moment had never come. Now she had her chance to make the difference. (2002)

- ◆ *Write a short story* using **ONE** of the following titles:

  The Stranger   The Fog   Into the Darkness (2003)
- ◆ *Write a short story* entitled: The Attic (2003)
- ◆ *Write a short story* in which a mobile phone plays an important part. (2004)
- ◆ *Write a short story* about a character who is isolated from society. (2004)

Discursive Writing

The particular sections of the Credit GRC that apply here tell you to *'convey information, selecting and highlighting what is most significant'* You have to be able to *'marshal ideas and evidence in support of an argument'* and these ideas should have *'depth and some complexity'* As you argue you need to show that you are *'capable of objectivity, generalisation and reasoning'* To be able to do this, you need to be able to use facts and experiences to back up and strengthen the opinions you express.

Fact and opinion

A **fact** is something you can check, measure or prove. Facts are correct and accurate. It should not be possible for two people to disagree about a fact. For example:

> Lemons are yellow

> Madonna is a singer

An opinion is something connected to your ideas and feelings about a subject. Different people will have different opinions about the same subject. Opinions often cause arguments. For example:

> Lemons are horrible

> Madonna is a good singer

For Practice

Read these sentences. Decide if they are facts or opinions. The answers are at the back.

1 That car over there is red.

2 Celtic is a football team.

3 All drugs have an effect on you.

4 It's wrong to carry out research using live animals.

5 George W. Bush is a bad president.

6 Abortion is always wrong.

7 School is boring.

8 Red cars look more sporty and fast.

9 The law permits abortion in some circumstances.

10 People who understand computers are nerds.

11 Computers are important in society today.

12 Celtic is a rubbish football team.

13 George W. Bush was elected in 2000.

14 All drugs are bad for you.

15 Some medical research uses live animals.

A good piece of discursive writing will use facts and personal experiences to back up opinions and make them seem reasonable.

For Practice

Printed below is a news article. You are going to search through it for facts, opinions, and experiences. If you are happy to write on this book or if you can photocopy the page you can do this by using three different colours. Use one colour to highlight or underline the facts. Use a second colour to do the same for the experiences, and a third one to show where the writer is expressing an opinion.

A few years ago my wife accompanied me on a trip to India. She saw the shrivelled people, the squalid huts, the children defecating in public. I knew what she was thinking. 'People shouldn't have to live this way'

The belief of most Europeans and Americans is that there shouldn't be poor people. Yet in much of Asia, Africa, and South America it is presumed normal for many people to be poor. The Bible tells us that the poor will always be with us.

It is not difficult to see how these attitudes developed. Throughout history, many people have felt that they were fortunate if they lived long enough to have their own children.

It is clear however that very few people want to be poor. The point of being called a 'developing' country is to let others know that you are trying to get rid of poverty. There is a one way movement in the world away from primitive tribal cultures towards modern, Westernised societies.

So, if nobody wants to be poor, why are there still poor people? One view is that people are poor because society is unjust and unfair. Poor people work incredibly hard, but get nowhere because society is set up not to reward them. Wicked governments often make the situation in poor countries worse.

This does not explain why there seem to be very poor people in very rich countries. In some communities it is shocking behaviour by the residents which makes life so hard. Stable families, a willingness to work, and respect for education and law are needed to improve these situations. Consider the communities where disputes are solved by shootings, where children are abandoned by their fathers and where drugs are openly traded. Is it any wonder that banks and shops close their doors?

The solution is to recognise that riches do not come naturally. Both society and people's own values have to change to get rid of poverty.

Planning two-sided pieces

Most Discursive Writing tasks you will tackle will be two-sided and will be about topics where there is some sort of disagreement or controversy. You will recognise these topics in the exam because they will contain an instruction to **Discuss**, or because you may be asked to look at both **advantages and disadvantages**. In these essays you should show that you understand the arguments on both sides, and at the end you can give your opinion.

There are two structures you can use to write two-sided Discursive essays. The simple one works like this:

Step 1 A one paragraph introduction to the topic.

The topic of school uniform is always a controversial one. Broadly speaking, parents and teachers seem always to be in favour of it, while the pupils who actually have to wear uniform are usually strongly opposed to it.

Step 2 A link sentence, explaining which side of the argument you will begin with.

Despite being a pupil and a therefore a victim of the craze for uniformity, I feel it's fair to begin by looking at the reasons why adults believe it to be such a good thing.

Step 3 All the points on one side of the argument. Each point should be in a separate paragraph, and wherever possible these points should be backed up with

facts or personal experiences. Start with the strongest, most convincing arguments and work your way down to the weaker ones.

Perhaps the strongest argument for making young people wear uniform at school is that this provides practise for the world of work. Anyone who goes on to work in a supermarket, a hotel, a restaurant or bank will almost certainly be required to wear the company uniform. Most offices have dress codes. Lawyers wear wigs and gowns, doctors wear scrubs or white coats, and actors wear costumes. Even the fashion-mad girls who most hate wearing what the school chooses find that as soon as they are at work in Oasis or Whistles they can wear only what their store sells. Far from being individuals they are reduced to being walking adverts. If this all goes on in real life, we may as well get used to it in school.

Step 4 Link sentence showing that you are about to switch to the other side of the argument

I want to turn now to the other side of the argument, and to voice the thoughts of pupils who do not wish to look as if they were all cut out of the same roll of cloth.

Step 5 Now do the same on this side of the argument as you did at **Step 3** above, working from stronger points down to weaker ones.

Step 6 Finally, in your conclusion, briefly sum up what you have written. Now say which side you agree with and why. Show which arguments convinced you, or refer to an experience in your life or the life of someone you know which has convinced you that a particular side is right.

It is clear that both the pro and anti uniform camps have strong arguments. Having looked at both sides I am forced to agree that on the whole it benefits pupils to wear school uniform. I realise that when I put on my uniform I put on my school attitude and mindset, and it's part of what makes me ready for the working day. Of course I still feel tremendous relief when I take it off, but I'm forced to admit that wearing the uniform probably helps me perform better at school.

The more complex structure for two-sided pieces makes you look more skilled at handling your material. It works like this:

The introduction and conclusion are the same as they are in an essay using the simple structure. However in the main body of the essay, you begin with the strongest argument from one side of the argument. Then, in the next paragraph, you work through a point on the opposite side which contradicts what you have just written about.

Perhaps the strongest argument for making young people wear uniform at school is that this provides practise for the world of work . . . If this all goes on in real life, we may as well get used to it in school.

However school is not the world of work. Pupils are not being paid to turn up, and in fact even have to pay for uniforms at school, when in the outside world many employers provide company clothing for free. Also, while there is a strong argument for kitting out business staff smartly to deal with clients, school pupils do not have customers.

Then take the second strongest point from the first side of the argument. Explain it, and then challenge it by making another point from the opposite side which could be said to contradict it. Keep going, following this pattern.

You may find that some of your points cannot be paired up in this way. If you still feel they are valuable and want to use them, then you can deal with them just before you start your conclusion. All the remaining points can be rolled into two short paragraphs, one for the ideas which support one side of the argument, for example:

There are some other good reasons why many people believe pupils should wear school uniform . . .

and the other for the evidence that matches the other side of the argument, for example:

Those who are against the wearing of uniform also have some further reasons for their position . . .

Planning one-sided pieces

More rarely, you will get the opportunity to write a one-sided piece. This is often referred to as **Persuasive Writing**. In this situation you should be dealing with a topic which you are personally interested in and knowledgeable about. The key here is to use facts and experiences to put across a series of points to support something you believe. Your aim is to persuade the reader to agree with you.

This type of approach often works well with topics which are of personal importance, and where you can display wit, irony or even sarcasm. 'Why chart music is rubbish' is an ideal subject here for example, whereas the rights and wrongs of more serious topics need the two-sided approach outlined above.

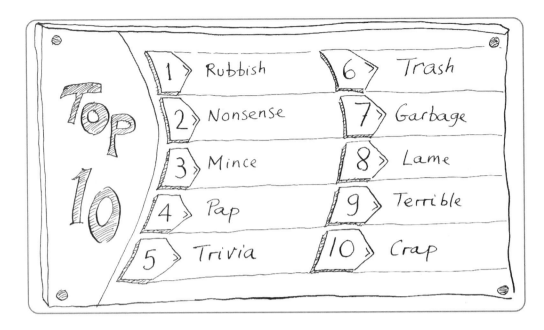

Overdone topics

There are some topics which come up again and again. Markers get very tired of reading about certain subjects. What is more, they have probably read all the arguments before, and will quickly notice if you miss out anything they expect to find, or if there is any important aspect of the argument which you do not explore carefully enough.

The two most overdone topics are **abortion** and **animal testing**. Unless you are truly an expert on one of these, steer clear of writing about these subjects. If you do feel compelled to tackle one of these issues, make sure you do it in a two sided way, and that you give each side a fair workout before presenting your own opinion at the end. Otherwise you run the risk of sounding like a fanatical zealot.

Direction markers

There are certain words and phrases which can be used to signal the direction of the argument in a piece of discursive writing, or to emphasise the writer's point of view. You will find most of these words and phrases at the start of a paragraph or sentence.

Look at the three headings below:

◆ These words and phrases move the argument forwards.

◆ These words and phrases let the argument change direction.

◆ These words and phrases are used in summing up.

Look at the group of words and phrases in the box. Each one fits best under one of those headings. Put each heading at the top of a piece of paper. Underneath the heading, jot down the words that fit there. If there are any words in the box that you are not familiar with, check them with a dictionary. You can check the answers at the back of the book.

thus	otherwise	moreover	yet
nevertheless	finally		on the contrary
likewise	conversely		on the other hand
unquestionably	therefore	however	next
despite	similarly	in spite of	absolutely
at the same time	without question		and
in retrospect	without doubt	significantly	
in conclusion	first(ly)	accordingly	
also	in brief	second(ly)	although
	in addition	furthermore	as a result
consequently	third(ly)	because	
	on the whole	to sum up	

For Practice

Here are some tasks from recent Writing Exams which involve producing a discursive piece. Pick one and try to write it. Remember to give yourself just an hour and a quarter in total, and to follow the time structure you saw at the end of chapter four. Try to include facts as well as opinions.

◆ 'Children aren't children for long these days. They are in too much of a hurry to grow up.' Is this a fair statement? **Discuss.** (2001)

◆ Designer sports gear – nothing more than a fashion statement? A waste of money? **Discuss** (2002)

◆ The natural world is in danger if we do not take steps to protect it. **Write your views.** (2003)

◆ Violence on the screen encourages violence in real life. **Discuss.** (2003)

◆ The more television channels there are, the harder it is to find something good to watch. **Do you agree or disagree? Give your views.** (2004)

◆ The Internet continues to make the world smaller. **Write about the advantages and disadvantages** of the Internet. (2004)

Writing Newspaper Reports

Newspaper reports follow a particular set of rules and guidelines. Some of these rules outline the way the piece is written, others cover the layout.

Writing rules

The first paragraph, or early paragraphs, outline the main subject of the article.

Later paragraphs go into the subject in more detail.

When quotations are used, people with the strongest personal connection to the story speak earlier in the article. Experts, commentators, and people with a less strong personal connection are quoted later.

The headline may use alliteration, rhyme or reference to well-known phrases to catch the reader's attention.

Layout rules

The writing is set out in columns.

There is a headline above the article

A photograph may be used to illustrate the article

The journalist's name (known as the byline) appears either at the start or the end of the article.

A caption is used to explain what the photograph shows.

For Practice

Read the following newspaper report. How many of the features listed above can you spot?

Teenage Tanorexics

It took only a few weeks of dedicated sunbed-worshipping for Tony Cowan's skin to turn from ghost-white to sumptuous honey. Over the same short period, he felt his personality had also been transformed by the rays of the tanning salon. He no longer felt shy, introverted and ugly. Instead, he became confident, sociable and started to like what he saw in the mirror.

He was 13 at the time. 'At first I told my mum it came from a bottle because she would have killed me if she knew I was going for a sunbed every day,' he said. 'I used my lunch money. Sometimes I would tell my mum I was going to the cinema so that I could get extra money.'

Tony, who is now 15, is one of a growing number of teenagers thought to be suffering from 'tanorexia'. Last week, 13-year-old Hayley Barlow from Liverpool spoke about her addiction to sunbeds, saying she felt 'transparent' if she did not have a daily dose.

The British Medical Association and Cancer Research UK have called for a ban on under–16s using the salons and experts warned that an obsession with tanning has become common among teenage girls. What was not mentioned was the increasing number of teenage boys across Britain who are also dedicating themselves to the pursuit of the perfect tan.

'These days everybody goes for sunbeds,' said Tony, who suggested that if I stood outside his school in Glasgow I would think I was in St Tropez. 'Loads of boys use them. Some girls prefer fake tan now because they are worried about the health risks. But a bottled tan is a waste of time. It makes them look orange. A sunbed tan is nicer and more natural.'

Tony has not gone without a sunbed for more than three days over the past three years despite his mother's warnings about the dangers. 'If I don't go for a few days I just feel kind of ugly and can't go out', he says.

Dr Linda Papadopoulos, a psychologist and author of *Mirror Mirror: The Body Image Revolution*, said there was considerable pressure on adolescents to conform to the images of perfection with which they are bombarded.

'Looking good has become so important to a teenager's sense of self-esteem. Teenagers convince themselves they can't get the girl or boy they want unless they have a good tan or are a certain weight. I don't think it's an addiction. It's more like a security blanket.'

Professor John Hawk, consultant dermatologist at St Thomas's Hospital in London, has a special interest in the effects of sunlight on the skin and has treated patients who have developed cancers from chronic sunbed use.

'People under 16 should never use sunbeds. Sunbeds do the same damage as sunlight and people who spend time on them risk ending up with old, dry, wrinkly, itchy skin with blotches all over it and in a proportion of people, skin cancer as well.'

Tony is aware of the risks but said he preferred not to think about them. 'I just wouldn't like to contemplate life without a suntan.'

Lorna Martin

Writing headlines

The job of a headline is to attract the reader's attention. A front page headline may even convince someone to buy a particular paper and headlines on other pages are there to make you want to read the article that follows. Headline writers, especially those working for tabloid papers, love using word tricks to achieve this effect.

In this book you will find news stories on pages 52 and 159. Both of these use *alliteration* in their headlines. This is a very common tactic. For example, a football story about an Edinburgh derby game could have the headline:

Happy Hearts Hammer Hopeless Hibees

Headline writers are also fond of puns; jokes based on the sounds of words. One of the most famous headlines of all time went with a report of a genuine football match in which, against all odds, Inverness Caledonian Thistle beat Celtic in a Scottish Cup match. The headline, based on the song 'Supercalllifrajilisticexpiallidocious' from the film *Mary Poppins* said:

Super Cally Go Ballistic Celtic are Atrocious

Watch a TV news bulletin and make up alliterative headlines for the top five stories.

Differences between the Folio and the Exam

Newspaper Writing is the only genre that you should tackle in two different ways, depending on whether you are doing the task as a Folio piece or in the Exam. If you are writing a newspaper report as a Folio piece you will have the luxury of plenty of time, and you should make sure you follow all the rules, including the layout ones. You should set out the headline in larger lettering at the top of the article and put in a picture. (You do not have to draw this yourself: you can stick on one you have cut out from somewhere else.)

However in the exam you can not afford to do anything that will waste your precious time, of which you have so little. You must follow the writing rules, and you can also quickly draw a line down the centre of the exam booklet to set your text out in a couple of columns. You should give the piece a headline, so that you can show off your ability to copy the style of headline writers, but you don't need to spend time producing big letters. Writing it at the top of the page in capitals will be enough. What you should **not** spend time on is drawing pictures – not all newspaper reports have one anyway, and this is an English exam, not an Art one.

For Practice

Here are some tasks from recent Writing Exams which involve producing a newspaper report. Pick one and try to write it. Remember to give yourself just an hour and a quarter in total, and to follow the time structure you saw earlier in this chapter.

◆ **Write a newspaper report** using the headline: Street Sealed Off! (2001)

◆ **Write a newspaper report** with the title: Winner Takes All (2002)

◆ Storm Damage Widespread **Write a newspaper report** using this headline. (2003)

Descriptions

Although it is unlikely you will be asked to write a Descriptive piece as a Folio task, Descriptive Writing tasks are common in the Exam. You will usually find these on the back page of the booklet, where quotations (often from poems) are used to inspire you to describe a scene. There were some examples of these in Chapter 4.

A good piece of descriptive writing allows the reader to 'see' pictures in their mind. Some kind of atmosphere or mood will be created to make the reader feel involved.

For Practice

1 Write a description of what it would be like to wait for a long time at a bus stop on either a hot summer day or a cold winter day. Bring all your senses into your description.

2 Cut a picture of a person out of a magazine. It should not be a famous person, or anyone whose name you know. Characters in adverts are ideal for this task. Write a few paragraphs to introduce that character. Don't just describe their looks, try to infer their personality, job, and background from the way they look.

3 Look at the following two boxes of words. You will see adjectives in the box on the left and nouns on the right.

iron	old	apple	sledge
bouncy	mysterious	cd	smile
furry	clockwork	sandwich	story
scary	flaming	teapot	flute
fancy	disordered	mountain	spaghetti
spiral	twinkling	necklace	star
rough	incredible	room	pool
complex	magic	goldfish	scarf
icy	decorated	child	ghost
square	unending	balloon	dustbin

Run your pencil through the left hand box with your eyes shut. Stop at random to **pick an adjective**. Do the same with the right hand box to **pick a noun**.

You will now have a combination, for example 'decorated child' or 'iron apple'. Describe the thing the words have given you. You can repeat this task as often as you like to keep practising descriptions.

For Practice

Here are some tasks from recent Writing Exams which involve writing a Description. Pick one and try to write it. Remember to give yourself just an hour and a quarter in total, and to follow the time structure you saw earlier in this chapter.

◆ **Describe** a person you know who is interesting, but different. (2000)

◆ **Describe the scene** suggested by **one** of the following:

The sea is calm tonight
The tide is full, the moon lies fair
Upon the straits

OR

The fair breeze blew, the white foam flew
The furrows followed free;
We were the first that ever burst
Into that silent sea.   (2002)

◆ **Describe the scene** brought to mind by **one** of the following:

A ship is floating in the harbour now
A wind is overing o'er the mountain's brow

OR

The woods are lovely, dark and deep

OR

All shod with steel
We hissed along the polished ice (2003)

◆ **Write a description** of your ideal home.   (2004)

Letters

There are certain very strict rules for the layout of a letter. Whether you write a letter for your Folio or in the Exam, the marker will expect you to follow these rules.

For Practice

To see whether you know the rules for letter layout, answer the questions below. You will find the solutions at the back of the book.

◆ All letters should start with the sender's address. Where does it go?

◆ What else would go just beneath the address?

Now let's think about the greeting at the start:

◆ How do you start a letter to your friend Tony?

◆ How would you start one to Tony Blair?

◆ How would you start one to an important stranger if you did not know their name?

Finally, you need to know how to end your letter. Match the proper ending to the person receiving the letter:

Yours sincerely	Tony Blair
Yours faithfully	your friend Tony
Lots of love	an important stranger

In the Writing Exam, some of the Letter Writing tasks will make you write **formal** letters, and some are about writing **informal** letters. You must be able to tell them apart because this affects the content of the letter.

For Practice

Look at the following letter tasks from past exams. Which are formal and which are informal?

◆ Imagine you are a new recruit to the army. Write a letter to your family or to a close friend describing you first week's experiences.

◆ Imagine you live on the top floor of a block of flats. Write a letter to your local housing authority complaining about the breakdown of the lift and the lack of security.

◆ Imagine you have had the opportunity to swim with a dolphin. Write to a close friend to describe the experience.

◆ Write to a pen friend, explaining the ups and downs of British weather and how it plays a huge part in our lives.

◆ You disapprove of circuses because you think they are cruel to animals. Write a letter to your local newspaper to explain your objections.

◆ Write a letter to your local director of Recreation and Leisure suggesting better facilities for sports in your area.

The body of the Letter will vary depending on whether it is informal or formal. Informal Letters should be friendly and chatty. Formal Letters, depending on the task, will usually be like the W1 pieces in your folio, either giving information or arguing opinions.

For Practice

Here are some tasks from recent Writing Exams which involve writing a letter. In fact these are the only two letter writing tasks at all in the five years from 2000 to 2004. It is a fairly rare kind of exam question. Pick one and try to write it. Remember to give yourself just an hour and a quarter in total, and to follow the time structure you saw at the end of chapter four.

◆ Some of our beaches and the sea are said to be no longer safe to use. **Write a letter** to a newspaper complaining about the state of a beach you have visited and making suggestions on how it can be improved. (2001)

◆ **Write a letter** to a local newspaper putting the case for more education for work. (2004)

Diaries

While you might write a Diary entry for your Folio, you are unlikely ever to do it in the Exam. In the last five years, only one Diary Writing task has appeared in the Writing Exam. The booklet showed a picture of an old-fashioned sailing ship trapped in ice, and candidates were asked to write one day's diary entry as it might be written by a member of the ship's crew.

If you write a Diary for your Folio, you may be asked to do this from your own point of view. However it is more likely in the Folio that you will be asked to do this as an Imaginative Response to Literature. For example, if you have studied Steinbeck's *Of Mice And Men*, you might be asked to produce a number of entries from George's diary as he writes about the time he and Lennie spend on the farm.

Apart from the convention of putting the date at the top of each entry, most of the rules for diary writing are the same as those for Personal Writing. The writer may use a little less reflection, as he or she is usually writing about very recent events and has not had much time to asses the effects of these. There should be a lot of use of thoughts and feelings, and of course a very strong pint of view. It can be quite fun to write the diary of a person who has done something wrong, but who strongly believes they did the right thing, or who wants to justify his or her actions.

TALK ASSESSMENT AND INDIVIDUAL TALK

Talk Assessment

Remember that one third of your total mark for the course comes from Talk. Your Talk grades are sent to the SQA along with your Folio in late March.

So, the good news is that you can do a lot to influence your final mark for English through this one part of the course. And, you never have to do a Talk exam! There will never be a day when a dull grey person in a dull grey suit appears in your classroom with a scary clipboard, sits right in front of you and waits for you to impress them.

The even better news is that your teachers DO get examined on Talk. Every few years they will be asked to watch videos of pupils talking, and to mark the Individual Talks and Group Discussions that they see. If the grades they give (mostly) agree with what the SQA has already decided, then your teachers have passed.

There is a downside too. You are unlikely to get any opportunity to choose what you talk about and almost certainly won't have a choice of Group Discussion topics. Nor is it likely that you'll be able to choose when you are assessed. On certain days, at certain times, you'll just have to be ready to perform, and you'll need to have all your skills in place. Finally, some people just feel very nervous about Talks, especially solo ones. This chapter will help you focus on the skills you will need for those days when you are assessed, and will also give you hints for overcoming or hiding your nerves.

Individual Talk

The Credit GRC expect you to give an Individual Talk of *'considerable length'* and which is made up of ideas of *'quality, relevance and distinction'*. This means you have a lot of work to do preparing your Talk, and getting all that prepared material into a format you can easily use.

Preparing Your Talk

The best way to use this section on Individual Talks is to prepare a talk as you read the next few pages. If you have a Talk coming up in school you can plan for that. If you do not know when your next Talk assessment will be, but you want to use this section now anyway, try to prepare a talk about a memorable or important experience you have had.

The first step is to follow the outline for the chosen Talk, writing out all the material that you want to use. Most of the suggested talks have lists of bullet points or questions to help you. You can write out what you want to say under each of these headings.

Good openings

Look at the two openings below. Which one do you think belongs to the General Talk, and which one begins a Talk that got Credit?

'Doctors, nurses, patients . . . As you've probably guessed I spent my work experience week in a hospital.'

'I'm going to talk about my week's work experience. I spent my time at a hospital.'

You should have spotted that the first one is the Credit one. The distinctive difference is that the Credit speaker draws the audience in, intrigues them, and immediately starts painting pictures in the listeners' heads, while the General speaker starts by saying something everyone probably knows already.

For Practice

Look back at the notes you have so far for the Talk you are preparing. Rewrite your opening to have more impact on the audience.

TALK ASSESSMENT AND INDIVIDUAL TALK

Varying vocabulary

You will find a whole section on this on the Writing chapters of this book. Just a quick reminder then that you have to vary your vocabulary in Talk, too. The GRC ask you to use *'varied and accurate vocabulary'* and to use *'a wide range of spoken language structures'* which means varying the lengths and types of sentences you use as well.

For Practice

Look back at the notes you have so far for the Talk you are preparing. Check over your vocabulary. Are there places where you could vary words? Remember variety can mean both avoiding boring repetition and also showing the breadth of your word choice.

As well as generally varying your vocabulary, there are other verbal techniques you can use to engage your audience and give impact to your talk.

Humour and anecdote

One of the easiest ways to win over your audience is to give them something to laugh at – especially if that something is you. Being funny to order may sound like a hard thing to do, but we all make our friends laugh all the time in real life by using **anecdotes**. An anecdote is an amusing story, often one we tell about, or even against, ourselves.

Let's imagine you have been asked to give a Talk about a childhood memory. You might start it like this:

> 'I'm going to talk to you today about the first time I went away without my parents. I was just ten when I went away to Cub camp.'

Or you might start it like this:

'I've never forgotten my first Cub camp. It started pretty badly. I had just managed to prise my weeping mother off me at the scout hut door. I was on my way in to join my Irn Bru crazed wee pals when she appeared again. To my horror she was waving the teddy bear I had had since birth and yelling at full pitch, "Darling you forgot Mr Snuggly and I know you never go to bed without him!'

 Which opening is more likely to capture your listeners?

Although anecdotes are especially useful in personal talks you do not have to personally star in each one that you use. An anecdote can just as easily be something you observed, or an experience that you know happened to someone else.

Exaggeration

You may have noticed that if you tell a particularly good anecdote more than once it tends to grow in the telling. Imagine you are on the bus on your way to meet some friends at the cinema, and a drunk gets on and sits in the seat behind you. When you tell your friends about this in the ticket queue it might sound like this:

'He absolutely reeked of cheap lager. Once or twice he even waved the can at me. He kept talking to me. I was glad to get off the bus.'

By the time you tell another friend about it on the phone later it might sound like this:

> 'He totally stank. The lager fumes were coming off him in waves. Then it got worse. He waved the can at me and said, "Come on hen, you'll take a wee drink"?'

If you meet someone else the next day, the anecdote might have grown into this:

> 'The smell coming off him was phenomenal. I promise you I could see the lager fumes hanging in the air between us. I practically had to flatten myself against the window to get away from him, but he still wouldn't leave me alone. Then he actually held the can up to my lips and slurred out, "Come on darlin' have a drink on me" I couldn't help it. I had to take a sip'

The third version may bear a bit less relation to the truth, but it's a much better anecdote, and one that you can really liven up in the telling.

For Practice

Go back to your notes again. This time, amend them to put in one or two anecdotes, exaggerating where you can to create humour.

Rhetorical questions

Let's go back to the student who was talking about her work experience in a hospital. Look at the following two sentences she could use:

> 'I'm sure some of you would feel sick if you had to watch an operation.'

> 'How would you feel if you had to watch a surgeon doing an operation?'

The second sentence is an example of a ***rhetorical question***. The speaker does not expect anyone to answer, but the audience understands this. Nobody is going to stand up and interrupt her by saying, 'A bit sick actually, since you're asking.'

What the question does is makes the audience feel involved. They go beyond just listening to your Talk and start involving themselves in it, thinking about your situation and sympathising with you.

For Practice

Go back to your Talk notes. Try to find a couple of places where you could change statements into rhetorical questions.

Emotive language

Of the particular techniques we have looked at so far, **anecdote** and **exaggeration** are especially useful in personal Talks, and in Talks where humour is appropriate. Rhetorical questions can be useful in all sorts of Talks. One technique that can be particularly helpful in serious or persuasive Talks in to use emotive language.

As we have seen in the Reading chapter, emotive words are strong ones, ones that rouse the listeners' emotions. If you listen to politicians (especially those on the opposition side), or if you read the advertising sent out by charities, you will often find a lot of emotive language in use.

Some emotive language aims to cause negative emotions such as anger or disgust.

For Practice

Look at the words in the box on the left. How many similar ones could you add to the box on the right?

disgusting	terrible
appalling	shocking
vile	dreadful

Some emotive language aims to cause more positive emotions.

For Practice

Look at the words in the box on the left. How many similar ones could you add to the box on the right?

fantastic	wonderful
amazing	marvellous
fabulous	great

Good endings

Endings matter too. Lots of speakers just stop. They make their last point, and then come to a halt, leaving the audience wondering if this is just an awkward pause and whether there's more to come.

Remember

The very final words of your Talk should make it clear that you are finished. You could use phrases like:

'Thank you for listening.'

'Does anyone have any questions?'

'I hope that you enjoyed hearing about . . .'

As well as these final sentences, you should use the whole of the last section of your Talk – the last card of your notes – to let the audience know that you are building up to a conclusion. If you are talking about a hobby, you could sum up what you enjoy most about it. If you are talking about a film or a book, again you could give an overall opinion. If your Talk is about a personal experience, you could sum up how you think this experience has affected you, or why you think you still remember it so clearly. In other words, you can use all the reflective techniques we found out about in the Personal Writing section of the Writing chapter.

For Practice

Look back at the notes you have so far for the Talk you are preparing. Rework your ending.

Using notes

The GRC do not say anything about using notes. However they do say that you have to **'make appropriate use of eye contact . . . and gesture'**, and the way you handle your notes can affect these.

HOW TO PASS STANDARD GRADE ENGLISH

> ### Hints *and* Tips
>
> **Your notes are there to support you if you need them. You should never just read your Talk out – this is not what you are being marked on. The best way to avoid this is to keep your notes as short as possible, so that you *can't* just read them.**

Let's imagine you're doing a Talk about your work experience, and that you spent the week at a hospital. You might want to say something like this:

> As soon as I arrived on the first day I was given a white coat and a hospital ID card. This made me feel as if I belonged. Once I put the coat on I thought I looked as if I could be a medical student. In fact I began to worry that I looked too good. What if one of the consultants suddenly asked me to take blood or put in some stitches?

If you get up to give your Talk with all these words written out, you may just read them. You need to reduce them to key words. You can start by underlining or highlighting the most important words and phrases.

As soon as I arrived on the ***first day*** I was given a ***white coat*** and a hospital ***ID*** card. This made me feel as if I ***belonged***. Once I put the coat on I thought I looked as if I could be a ***medical student***. In fact I began to ***worry*** that I looked too good. What if one of the consultants suddenly asked me to take ***blood*** or put in some ***stitches***?

If you speak from notes like these, however, you may still have to do a fair bit of scanning to find your key words. The next step is to write them out on small cards or slips of paper. Using strong colours and large print, write out your key words. You can also use layout to show the connections between ideas. Your card might now look like this:

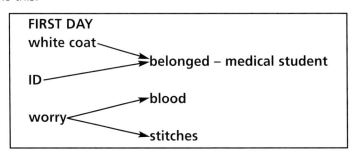

By the time you get to this stage, you will know your material so well that a quick glance down at these few words will bring up all you want to say.

For Practice

Go back to your notes. You should be able to set your whole talk out on cards, using colour, key words and simple symbols to bring everything quickly to mind.

Delivering Your Talk

Using props

It can be a very good idea to use props in your Talk. For instance if you are talking about a sport you play, you could bring some of the clothing or equipment.

If you are talking about a personal experience, you could bring some object associated with that memory.

Holding a prop gives you something to do with your hands, which may help you control signs of nerves. Passing a prop around is interesting for the audience and connects you more strongly to them. If your Talk is well prepared, then using props may remind you of everything you want to say, and help you to speak without notes

HOW TO PASS STANDARD GRADE ENGLISH

> ### For Practice
>
> Go back to your prepared Talk. Is there a prop you could use in your delivery?

Using PowerPoint and other technology

If your school is well equipped, you may be able to use a PowerPoint presentation to accompany your Talk. Your teacher may even actually ask you to try doing this in one of your Talks.

A word of warning here. Many PowerPoint users make a classic mistake. Instead of talking to the audience, they just read out what can be seen on the screen.

Remember you are not being graded on how well you can read aloud, but on how well you talk to the audience and engage their interest. If you are going to use PowerPoint, or prepare overheads to put up on a projector, they should add something extra that you cannot say in words. For example, they are an ideal way to show pictures or diagrams, but the fewer words you put on them the less you risk just reading something your listeners can see and read for themselves.

Hints and Tips

You shouldn't use PowerPoint, or any other technological prop, unless you are absolutely sure how it works. Even if you know how it would run on your computer at home, even if you know how to bring up a clip on your own video or DVD, make sure you get a chance to set up and practise on the equipment you'll be using at school.

Eye contact

The GRC say that a Credit student, *'makes appropriate use of eye contact.'* But what is appropriate?

If you have produced good notes as discussed already, then you are on your way to good eye contact, because you should not **need** to keep looking down. If you feel that you might **want** to keep looking down, there's a section coming up on dealing with nerves that you will find helpful. If you want to look up, but you are not sure how to, keep reading.

Your teacher will probably be sitting in the audience, making notes so that he or she can grade your Talk. Lots of pupils make the mistake of staring at the teacher. Some others look at their best friend in the class, because they know that person will support them. Others just look straight ahead.

Hints and Tips

Imagine you are a lighthouse. Although you are standing still, your eyes – the lamp of the lighthouse – can move, sweeping across the class like the light sweeps across the sea. Whenever you are able to look up for a few seconds, sweep your eyes across the class, taking in most of the room. You might notice that this is what your teachers do when they talk to their classes. The reason this works so well is that it makes everyone in the audience feel they should pay attention to you all the time, because they know you could look at them at any second.

Body language

The Credit GRC expect you to make *'good use of facial expression and gesture.'*

For Practice

Think of a TV presenter who is good at their job. (It should be someone who stands up to speak, and doesn't just read from a prepared script, so not a newsreader.) Now try watching them with the TV sound muted so you can focus on only what they do and not what they say. Make a list of the gestures they use. Can you work out, from their gestures alone, what they are talking about, or how they feel?

You should find that the TV presenter's body language helps him or her to put across the message. Unfortunately, bad body language can also lower your mark, and there are a few things to avoid.

Hints and Tips

Some people fidget terribly. All sorts of 'head' fidgets, like earring twisting, ear rubbing, nose scratching and hair twiddling are really your subconscious mind trying to send your hands to cover your mouth and stop you talking. These fidgets muffle what you say, and they display your nerves to the whole audience.

Some people, both girls and boys, hide behind their hair. If yours is long, tie it back.

Some people stand awkwardly, twisting their arms behind their backs or crossing their legs while standing up to Talk. I actually once saw someone tip over sideways because they'd crossed their legs! Try to plant your feet firmly, about shoulder-width apart.

Hints *and* Tips

If your classroom has a lectern or book stand, try putting your notes on that. You could even borrow a music stand and use it. This way you can lightly place your hands on the stand, and move them when you want to make a gesture. If you have to hold on to your notes, keep them in one hand and use the other for gestures.

 ### Engaging and creating a rapport with an audience

The best and really the only way to engage your audience is by doing an interesting talk that they feel they want to listen to. However there are a few other hints and tips to help you get the audience on your side:

- As mentioned above, one way to do this is by showing them something, or passing a prop round.

- Try asking them questions, not only rhetorical ones but perhaps also one where you clearly expect one or two of them to answer

- Get them to raise their hands to vote on something you have said, or to show that they have had a similar experience to the one you are describing, e.g. 'How many of you had a pet when you were young?'

HOW TO PASS STANDARD GRADE ENGLISH

◆ Give them the opportunity to ask you questions at the end

◆ Get them to laugh, and show them you appreciate that laughter by not talking over it

◆ Use language that includes them, e.g. 'I'm sure **we** have all at some point in **our** lives had to face something **we** were really frightened of.'

Dealing with nerves

Although we have left this to last, it is actually the first thing that comes to mind when many people find out they have to do a Talk. If you have prepared well, and taken on board all the advice I have given already, then that should help you to feel less nervous and more skilled. Another way to defuse nerves is to practise your Talk, on family, on friends, in the mirror or just alone in your room.

If you do practise on live volunteers, ask them to time what you say. Then ask them to tell you two things that were good about the Talk, and one you could improve.

Hints *and* Tips

Remind yourself that everyone in your audience probably has to do a Talk too and feels just the same way. If there is someone in the class that you really do not want to talk in front of, you could ask the teacher if that person could be asked to wait somewhere else while you make your speech to the class. You might find that asking to be assessed first and get it over with stops the nerves building up too much. Some teachers will even allow you to come at lunchtime or after school, and to bring a group of friends you feel comfortable with to be your audience.

For Practice

Now that you have planned your Talk and thought about the advice above, find an audience to practise on. Ask them for feedback, and then find a different audience and practise again.

TALK: GROUP DISCUSSION

If you have worked through the section on Individual Talk, then you already know most of what you need to do in Group Discussion too. Your contribution to the group has to be **'substantial'** and **'relevant'** in the words of the GRC, just as your Individual Talk will be.

What You Should Know

However the group situation does introduce a few differences:

◆ You will almost certainly have no choice of what you talk about. Your teacher will probably provide you with a discussion topic, a set of questions, or some other sort of group task.

◆ You probably won't get much of a chance to prepare your contribution, but will have to produce a good performance almost on the spot.

◆ You may or may not get to choose the other people who are in the group with you.

◆ You may be given a particular role to play in the group during the discussion.

◆ You need to show that you know how to behave in a group situation, which the marking scheme calls 'taking account of other contributors'.

We'll deal with particular group roles later. First, let's look at how body language and spoken language can be used to show that you are taking account of others.

For Practice

Imagine you had these two people in your group. Which person's body language shows that they are taking an active part in the group? Which one seems to have opted out?

So we can easily see how your body language shows that you are actively taking part. However you need to go beyond that. The GRC say that a Credit pupil, *'takes account of what others have to say in several of the following ways: by analysing, summarising, using, expanding, supporting, challenging, and refuting their contributions.'* (You should know what most of these words mean. 'Refuting' means proving that someone is wrong, so it is stronger than challenging, which might just involve asking them to justify their opinions and statements more fully.)

Remember

During the Discussion you should be doing more listening than talking. Listening does not mean staying quiet for as little time as possible until you can wedge in something that you have already decided to say. After all you have two ears and just one mouth. What you say when you speak should build on what you hear when you are listening. If you disagree with what you have heard, there are ways to express this without giving offence or seeming arrogant.

You may also notice that someone in your group is not contributing much, or is having trouble getting a word in because of more confident speakers hogging the conversation. If you can find a way to involve that quiet person, you're displaying a maturity and skill which will be rewarded.

For Practice

The comments in the speech bubbles fit into four groups.

◆ Some phrases keep the discussion going by letting you analyse or summarise what has been said so far.

◆ Some of them can show that you agree with the previous speaker and want to build on what they he or she has said.

◆ Some of them will let you express disagreement.

◆ Some are useful for involving others.

Can you work out which comments belong in which group? The answers are at the back.

Possible roles in groups

In some Group Discussions you may be asked to take on a certain role. Your teacher will mark how well you carry this out. Also, if others in your group have been given roles to play, you need to know what they should be doing so you know how to react to them.

If you are given a role, your teacher should make clear what is expected of you. Here are some of the more common roles:

Key Words and Definitions

The chairperson should lead the discussion and keep it moving along. The chair should also solve any conflicts or arguments and should try to encourage any shy group members while trying to stop confident speakers from dominating.

The leader has a similar role to the chair but may also be responsible for reaching a decision, or conclusion, or having the casting vote if the group cannot agree.

The reader may be asked to read out instructions, information or questions to the group.

The recorder takes notes of what is said. Near the end of the discussion it is a good idea to read your notes back to the group so that they can agree the reporter has kept a fair record.

The reporter may be asked to give a verbal report back to the whole class on what the group talked about.

The interviewer will ask questions. These may be given to the group, or the interviewer may have to make up the questions.

ANSWERS

Page 8

The vague, woolly tasks are the ones about *Dulce Et Decorum Est*, the first *Of Mice and Men* task, *To Kill A Mockingbird* and *Stone Cold*.

The tasks about character are *Uncle Ernest*, *Macbeth*, *Catcher In The Rye*, and *A Time To Dance*.

The tasks about theme are *Lord of the Flies* and the second *Of Mice And Men* task.

The task about the writer's style is *A Martian Sends A Postcard Home*.

The *Porphyria's Lover* task is a mixture of character and the writer's style.

Page 14

The first sentence '*The writer . . . mood*' makes a Point. The second sentence '*In the opening . . . spite*' provides Evidence. The last three sentences, '*We realise . . . murderous spite*' Explains the Effect on the reader.

Page 15

The quotation given at the start of the paragraph is the Evidence. The next section, '*Realising . . . in the whole book,*' Explains the Effect. The final sentence, '*Humanity . . . potential for evil,*' makes the Point.

Page 16

In the paragraph on page 14 the pupil refers back to the task instruction whenever he uses the word '*mood*' or '*moods.*'

Page 17

The paragraph should read like this. Any words changed have been printed in bold:

*When Holden **goes** to see his sister Phoebe he **shows** a different side of himself. Instead of being cynical he actually **shows** her how depressed he really **is**. It **is** obvious to me that Phoebe really **loves** him because she **is** so worried about him. When she **asks** Holden to make one thing he **likes** his only answer **is**:*

> *'I like Allie.'*

*This answer **helps** me to understand not just that he **is** depressed, but perhaps also why: the only thing he **likes is** the brother who **has** been dead for years.*

Page 22

1 'Like dogs to bark at our world.'

2 'I feared more than tigers.'

3 '. . . threw words like stones . . .'

4 .'. . . their salt coarse pointing . . .'

5 'their muscles like iron . . .'

Page 24

Porphyria's passion is personified when the narrator says that it would sometimes prevail, as to prevail means to win.

The feast is personified when he says that the feast was not able to restrain her.

Page 27

1 'dr**a**b pl**ai**d'

2 '**gr**oceries in **Gr**andfare bags'

3 'my **neighbour** and my **neighbour**'s child'

4 'her **d**inners smell **d**ifferent'

5 'drab'

6 '**g**old embroidered **g**orgeousness'.

7 'gold . . . golden'.

Page 28

The informal sections are, '*They fixed that stiff,*' and, '*I'll say it is.*' The extremely formal word is '*attired*'.

Page 29

The negative words in Local Colour are '*sullen*' and '*drab*'

The words connected to war, violence and the army in Timothy Winters are '*bombs*', '*blitz*', '*shoots*', and '*bombardier*'. As the '*Suez*' Canal was the site of a crisis in the 1950s involving the British army, this word could also join the list.

Page 31

By using so many words connected to war, violence and the army, Causley is saying that Timothy's life is a battle and that he has a really hard time. He may even be implying that Timothy suffers violence or physical abuse from his family, as well as the obvious neglect described.

Page 31

The words of cookery jargon are '*chop*', '*whip*', '*fluid ounces*', '*stiff peaks*', '*tablespoon*', '*separate*', '*dessertspoon*', '*whisk*', '*peaked*', '*bain Marie*', '*beat*', and '*folding*'.

Page 32

The words which the creators of The Lovers' Seat think are in Scottish dialect are '*canty*', '*ane anither*' and '*maun*'.

Page 33

The emotive words in the news story are '*shocking*', '*terrifying ordeal*', '*horrifying*', '*cruelly*', '*vicious*', '*appalling*', '*shocked*', '*foul*', '*evil*', '*petrified*', '*disturbing*', '*murderous*', '*sickened*', '*distraught*', '*suffering*', '*ridiculous*', '*hysterical*' and '*preposterous*'.

Page 34

The figure of speech used by the headline writer is alliteration.

Page 36

'too weak … struggling passions free'
'give herself … forever'
'sudden thought' 'gay feast'
'come through wind and rain'
'Porphyria worshipped'

Page 39

1H, 2D, 3G, 4B, 5F, 6A, 7E, 8I, 9C, 10J

Page 41

The phrases that tell you that you must quote from the passage in your answer are, '*Which word . . .*', '*Find an expression . . .*', '*Write down the word . . .*', and '*Which expression . . .*'.

Page 42 Answers to sample Reading Exam questions

The number of marks, and an explanation if necessary of how to award them, appears in bold after each answer or each part of more complex answers. In questions where you have not been asked to quote you do not need to use exactly the same words as the mark scheme, so long as your answer means the same thing.

Q 3 *Boxes – rickety or broken / baseball caps – free to start with / plastic dinosaurs – used or damaged / tattie-peeler – difficult to wash / plastic containers – ill-fitting lids / pancake mixer – splashes*

1 mark for each named and explained item

Q 4 *Reference to Victorian (novelist)* **(1)**

Reference to carriage **(1)**

Q 5 *To find out / see* **(1)**

if it was too scary/ frightening/ suitable for the boys **(1)**

Q 6 *(One vampire hand was) 'quite enough'* **(2)**

Q 7 *They felt they had to visit / it was their duty* **(1)**

because they were family / related **(1)**

They wanted to see **(1)**

what they were like **(1)**

Q 8 *(There was something) in her movements that was very tense* **(2)**

Q 9 *He pretended to be* **(1)** *a (puzzled) man looking for his wife / a man who'd lost his wife* **(1)**

Q 10 *bizarre* **(1)** *enigma* **(1)**

Q 11 *Something awful / dramatic was going to happen / it was gong to have tragic consequences / it was going to result in death / lead to extinction / it was going to be unlucky*

Any one of the above for 2 marks. Nothing for the idea of fate e.g. 'It was meant to happen'. *The* **important underlying idea is that the meeting led to the dodo's doom**

Q 12 *It appeared / seemed / looked* **(1)** *as if it would not work / as if it would not be any use* **(1)**

Q 15 *Because the man was interested / intended to apply / had been out of work for a year like the man in the advert / was attracted by the rewards*

1 mark each for any two of these answers

Q 16 *It was a busy place / had a working atmosphere* **(1)**

Which made it seem a better / luckier place to post it **(1)**

[Accept also a negative response based on the idea that the one in his street **(1)** *was unlucky* **(1)** *]*

Q 17 *ironic* **(2)**

comment e.g. they were afraid **(1)** *+ reference e.g. running away / went white* **(1)**

Q 18 *He was inquisitive / nosey / taking everything in* **(2)**

Q 19 *They were exaggerated / boastful OR the aunt was showing off / trying to impress / trying to belittle the mother*

Any of these answers for 2 marks

Q 20 *They wore clothing that was too big / loose* **(1)** *and could (easily) hide things* **(1)**

Q 21 *Their overcoats / briefcases* **(1)** *were good for hiding things* **(1)**

Q 22 *He wondered if people would think* **(1)** *that they were a couple shopping* **(1)**

He avoided going through the office area / went up the back stairs **(1)** *so she would not be seen / not be embarrassed* **(1)**

Q 24 *Misrepresented* **(2)**

Q 25 *Magnificent / thinks it is very beautiful / very attractive* **(2)**

Idea of intensity of her opinion must be present

Q 27 *(The word) gingerly is placed* **(1)** *at the start (of the sentence)* **(1)**

Q 28 *Each item* **(1)** *is given a sentence on its own* **(1)**

No marks for saying that the sentences are short: short sentences do not imply a short list

Q 29 *To show that the list could continue / be endless OR that there could be more examples* **2 marks for either answer**

Q 30 *To elaborate on an idea* **(2)**

Q 31 *To introduce an explanation* **(2)**

Q 32 *To provide additional information / detail / parenthesis* **(2)**

Q 33 *Being ironic / to show it's not really a castle / to show it's really a hotel* **(2)**

Q 34 *Giving additional information / parenthesis* **(2)**

Q 35 *Use of a / an / one / individual / solitary*

Any 2 for 1 mark each

Q36 *She is controlled/ precise/ deliberate/ calculating/ elegant/ contrived/ graceful/ attention-seeking/ self conscious/a show off/ a poser*

Any one for 2 marks

Q 37 *Answers should deal with the idea that 'sideline' = left out / excluded etc* **(1)**

AND *that 'face in a crowd' = anonymity / one of many / lost / unimportant etc* **(1)**

Q 38 *. . . 'as if her head might explode'. / 'It ripped out of her . . . prisoner for years.'*

Either of these for 1 mark + appropriate comment on the intensity of the image for 1 more mark

Q 40 *Taxidermy means stuffing* **(1)**

Reference to unsuccessful attempt to preserve the dodo **(1)**

Q 42 *Reference to any TWO of – use of colon (to introduce) / (a list of) examples / unwanted gifts / wee something for Christmas / birthday gift not wanted / holiday souvenirs / stuff / (which) clutters our lives / recycled rubbish*

1 mark for each

Q 43 *Reference to any TWO of: very small table / only one chair / which is an upright one / the window is barred (like a cell – possibly dark) / the only outlook is the fire escape / the wall-mounted phone*

1 mark each Nothing for mentioning the smallness of the room

Q45 *'In spite of this' refers to the lessons of the first paragraph.*

'. . . through the Racecourse fence' takes Howard in to the setting of the third paragraph.

1 mark for each quote + reference.

Page 69

In the example questions on page 67, Task 2 allows you to write personally.

Page 70

5 minutes   Choosing a task

5 minutes   Planning your writing

1 hour   Writing

5 minutes   Checking over your work

Page 71

Monday was fine and sunny. There wasn't a cloud in the sky and I spent the whole day sunbathing.

The next day was rainy and cold and I decided to go to the shops.

At Intersport I chose a pair of trainers, a sweatshirt and some tracksuit trousers.

When I went to pay the assistant said, 'That's two hundred pounds please.'

'How much?' I gasped.

'Two hundred pounds,' she repeated.

'Oh,' I gasped again. I dumped my shopping and ran off.

On the bus home I felt really stupid. Why had I come without money?

Suddenly, my fairy godmother appeared. 'I'll give you three wishes,' she said.

'Tracksuit trousers, trainers and sweatshirt please,' I replied.

Page 72

The two of them were on their way to the pictures when the argument broke out. Donna didn't want to see an action film. 'I hate them,' she moaned.

'Well I'm tired of always seeing romances,' answered Lesley.

'I don't care,' replied Donna. 'I want to see something that makes me feel happy inside.'

Suddenly Lesley said a very cruel thing. 'You only want to watch romantic films because there's no romance in your life. You haven't had a snog since we were in first year.'

'That's not true!'

'Yes it is!'

'I had a snog with Graham after the Christmas party last year!'

'No you didn't. You told everyone that you went off with him, but we all saw him at the bus stop on his own at the time when you said he was with you.'

This made Donna absolutely furious. 'At least I'm a bit choosy about who I snog. You've kissed so many guys your lips are fraying.'

Lesley couldn't think of anything to say in reply to this, and stormed off home in a huff.

Page 73

'I need a doctor!' screamed the woman as she rushed into Casualty.

'I'm a doctor!' yelled Dr Brown, hurtling down the hospital corridor. 'What seems to be the problem?'

'I've gone deaf,' said the woman. 'I woke up this morning and I wasn't able to hear anything out of my right ear. And,' she went on, 'it tickles.'

'Oh dear' said Dr Brown. 'That does sound nasty. Let me take a look at it.'

He led her into a consulting room and shone a bright light in her ear. 'Hmm, yes,' he muttered. 'Do you have any children madam?'

'I have a little boy, Liam. He's only four. But what has that got to do with my ears?'

'Did you make him have peas for dinner last night?'

The woman nodded. 'I did, but I still don't see what this has got to do with me going deaf.'

'And does he hate peas?'

'Yes but I still don't understand the connection.'

'Keep quite still,' said Dr Brown. 'You may feel an odd sensation but it shouldn't hurt.'

'Ow!' yelled the woman, who certainly appeared to think that it had hurt.

'Aha!' exclaimed Dr Brown. He showed her the point of a pen lid, on which perched a slightly waxy-looking pea. 'I think your son got his revenge while you were asleep.'

Page 77

A possible way to rewrite Item A could be:

I focused my lens to get a better look. The mums were pushing children on the swings and he leaned over the fence grinning. As I watched his every move I realised he was up to something.

Page 78

A possible way to rewrite Item A could be:

As I walked down the corridor to class on the first day at my new school I felt nervous but still excited. I wondered if anyone would like me and what they would think of me. Would I fit in?

Page 87

First person words: I, me, we, mine, us, our, my

Second person words: yours, you, your

Third person words: they, her, she, he, them, theirs, hers, his

Page 88–89

These are some suggested answers to the four questions. You can probably think of more.

◆ Opening number 1 is very repetitive and has many sentences starting with the word 'He . . .' We are told far too much information, most of which is unlikely to have any importance to what actually happens in the story, such as what he eats and drinks for breakfast.

◆ Opening number 2 is much shorter and gets to the point more quickly. The use of alliteration in the words '*dull*' and '*disastrous*' and the deliberate repetition of these words, attracts our attention. We want to know why his skive turns out to be a disaster.

◆ Some readers might find the repetition of the words 'dull' and 'disastrous' in Opening number 2 irritating.

◆ The final sentence, '*He would regret it later*,' grabs our attention and makes us wonder what is going to go wrong for Michael when he skives school.

Page 90

◆ The first two forbidden endings, the dream and the Lottery win, are lazy writing. Some writers who use them can't be bothered thinking of an ending to the story. Some writers realise too late that they have started a story which they cannot finish within a reasonable length, or a reasonable amount of time.

◆ The third ending, which summarises the rest of the characters' lives or a huge chunk of them, adds too much information. Look back to page 138 for guidelines about the simplicity of good short stories.

◆ '*Happily ever after*,' is just a cliché. Unless you are deliberately being ironic, or are actually writing a fairy tale, do not use it.

Page 91

The facts are sentences 1, 2, 3, 9, 11, 13 and 15. The other sentences are opinions.

Page 97

These words and phrases move the argument forwards:

likewise moreover unquestionably next similarly absolutely at the same time and without question without doubt significantly first(ly) also secondly in addition furthermore third(ly)

These words and phrases let the argument change direction:

otherwise yet nevertheless on the contrary conversely on the other hand however despite in spite of although

These words and phrases are used in summing up:

thus therefore in retrospect in conclusion accordingly in brief as a result consequently because on the whole to sum up finally

Pages 103

◆ The sender's address goes in the top right corner of the page

◆ The date goes beneath the address

◆ Dear Tony

◆ Dear Mr Blair

◆ Dear Sir or Madam

◆ Writing to a friend, you could end with, 'Lots of love'.

◆ Writing to Tony Blair, you should end with, 'Yours sincerely'.

◆ Writing to an important stranger, whose name you do not know, you should end with, 'Yours faithfully'.

Page 104

The formal letters are those about conditions in the block of flats, about circuses and about better sports facilities. The other letter choices are informal.

Page 123

These phrases keep the discussion going by letting you analyse or summarise what has been said so far.

So what you mean is . . .
So we've agreed that . . .
You seem to be saying that . . .
So we seem to be saying that . . .

These phrases can show that you agree with the previous speaker and want to build on what they he or she has said.

I agree with you because . . .
You're right to say that . . .
I'd like to add that . . .
That's a good idea . . .
I'm glad you suggested that . . .

These phrases will let you express disagreement.

I don't agree because . . .
I think you're wrong because . . .
I think you'll find that . . .
On the other hand . . .
In my opinion . . .
Actually I don't think . . .
I see your point but . . .
Actually what happens is . . .
I'm sorry but I think that . . .
That might be true but . . .
If you think more carefully you'll realise . . .
I'm afraid you're wrong because . . .

These phrases are useful for involving others.

What do you think . . .?
I'd like to hear from X . . .
What's your opinion . . .?
What would you like to say . . .?
Is there anything you'd like to add . . .?
Can you explain . . .?